GOVERNANCE
SERIES

FINANCIAL RESPONSIBILITIES

of Nonprofit Boards

Second Edition

Andrew S. Lang, CPA

BOARDSOURCE®
Building Effective Nonprofit Boards

Library of Congress Cataloging-in-Publication Data

Lang, Andrew S.

Financial responsibilities of nonprofit boards / Andrew S. Lang, -- 2nd ed.

    p. cm. -- (Governance series ; bk. 3)

ISBN 1-58686-108-5

1. Nonprofit organizations--Finance. 2. Directors of corporations.
I. Title.

    HG4027.65.L36 2008
    658.15--dc22   2008038858

© 2009 BoardSource.
First Printing, October 2008
ISBN 1-58686-108-5

Published by BoardSource
750 9th Street, NW, Suite 650
Washington, DC 20001-2521

BOARDSOURCE®

Building Effective Nonprofit Boards

BoardSource was established in 1988 by the Association of Governing Boards of Universities and Colleges (AGB) and Independent Sector (IS). Prior to this, in the early 1980s, the two organizations had conducted a survey and found that although 30 percent of respondents believed they were doing a good job of board education and training, the rest of the respondents reported little, if any, activity in strengthening governance. As a result, AGB and IS proposed the creation of a new organization whose mission would be to increase the effectiveness of nonprofit boards.

With a lead grant from the Kellogg Foundation and funding from five other donors, BoardSource opened its doors in 1988 as the National Center for Nonprofit Boards with a staff of three and an operating budget of $385,000. On January 1, 2002, BoardSource took on its new name and identity. These changes were the culmination of an extensive process of understanding how we were perceived, what our audiences wanted, and how we could best meet the needs of nonprofit organizations.

Today BoardSource is the premier voice of nonprofit governance. Its highly acclaimed products, programs, and services mobilize boards so that organizations fulfill their missions, achieve their goals, increase their impact, and extend their influence. BoardSource is a 501(c)(3) organization.

BoardSource provides

- resources to nonprofit leaders through workshops, training, and an extensive Web site (www.boardsource.org)

- governance consultants who work directly with nonprofit leaders to design specialized solutions to meet an organization's needs

- the world's largest, most comprehensive selection of material on nonprofit governance, including a large selection of books and CD-ROMs

- an annual conference that brings together approximately 900 governance experts, board members, and chief executives and senior staff from around the world

For more information, please visit our Web site at www.boardsource.org, e-mail us at mail@boardsource.org, or call us at 800-883-6262.

Have You Used These BoardSource Resources?

THE GOVERNANCE SERIES

1. Ten Basic Responsibilities of Nonprofit Boards, Second Edition
2. Legal Responsibilities of Nonprofit Boards, Second Edition
3. Financial Responsibilities of Nonprofit Boards, Second Edition
4. Fundraising Responsibilities of Nonprofit Boards, Second Edition
5. The Nonprofit Board's Role in Mission, Planning, and Evaluation, Second Edition
6. Structures and Practices of Nonprofit Boards, Second Edition

BOOKS

Understanding Nonprofit Financial Statements, Third Edition

The Nonprofit Policy Sampler, Second Edition

The Nonprofit Dashboard: A Tool for Tracking Progress

Financial Committees

Minding the Money: An Investment Guide for Nonprofit Board members

The Nonprofit Board Answer Book: A Practical Guide for Board Members and Chief Executives, Second Edition

The Nonprofit Chief Executive's Ten Basic Responsibilities

The Board Chair Handbook, Second Edition

Getting the Best from Your Board: An Executive's Guide to a Successful Partnership

Moving Beyond Founder's Syndrome to Nonprofit Success

The Source: Twelve Principles of Governance That Power Exceptional Boards

Exceptional Board Practices: The Source in Action

Fearless Fundraising for Nonprofit Boards, Second Edition

Navigating the Organizational Lifecycle: A Capacity-Building Guide for Nonprofit Leaders

Managing Conflicts of Interest: A Primer for Nonprofit Boards, Second Edition

Driving Strategic Planning: A Nonprofit Executive's Guide

Taming the Troublesome Board Member

The Nonprofit Legal Landscape

Self-Assessment for Nonprofit Governing Boards

The Nonprofit Board's Guide to Bylaws

Transforming Board Structure: Strategies for Committees and Task Forces

The Board Building Cycle: Nine Steps to Finding, Recruiting, and Engaging Nonprofit Board Members, Second Edition

Culture of Inquiry: Healthy Debate in the Boardroom

Chief Executive Transitions: How to Hire and Support a Nonprofit CEO

DVDs

Meeting the Challenge: An Orientation to Nonprofit Board Service

Speaking of Money: A Guide to Fundraising for Nonprofit Board Members

For an up-to-date list of publications and information about current prices, membership, and other services, please call BoardSource at 800-883-6262 or visit our Web site at www.boardsource.org.

CONTENTS

ABOUT THE BOARDSOURCE GOVERNANCE SERIES

As BoardSource celebrated its 20th anniversary in 2008, we introduced updated editions of the books in the Governance Series, BoardSource's flagship series created to help nonprofit board members understand their primary roles and responsibilities. BoardSource believes that board members and chief executives who know and understand their mutual responsibilities are better equipped to advance their organizations' missions and, in turn, strengthen their communities.

WHY IS A STRONG BOARD IMPORTANT?

There's no denying that the 1.6 million nonprofit organizations in the United States play a vital role in society, from assisting victims of natural disasters to beautifying our neighborhoods, from educating our children to healing the sick. To ensure that their organizations have the resources, leadership, and oversight necessary to carry out these and other vital activities, nonprofit boards must understand and fulfill their governance responsibilities.

Although there have been headline-worthy scandals by a few nonprofits and their boards, the vast majority try hard every day to be worthy of the public's trust. Nevertheless, BoardSource frequently hears from nonprofit board members and chief executives who say that they are not always sure what the basic components of good governance are or how to educate every board member in them so they can serve their organizations and the public in the best possible manner. The revised Governance Series helps bridge this gap in knowledge.

Within the board's broad roles of setting the organization's direction, ensuring necessary resources, and providing oversight, board members wear many hats. They are guardians of the mission; they ensure compliance with legal and financial requirements; and they enforce ethical guidelines for their organization. They are policymakers, fundraisers, ambassadors, partners with the chief executive, and strategic thinkers. They monitor progress, evaluate the performance of the organization and the chief executive, and demonstrate integrity in everything they do on behalf of the organization. Because of their many roles, board members need more than enthusiasm for a cause, passion for a mission, or just "good intentions." They need to understand all of their stewardship responsibilities and perform all of their duties.

WHAT WILL BOARD MEMBERS FIND IN THE BOOKS?

The six books address all of the fundamental elements of service common to most boards, including board member responsibilities, how to structure the board in the most efficient manner, and how to accomplish governance work in the spirit of the mission of the organization.

1. *Ten Basic Responsibilities of Nonprofit Boards, Second Edition* (Book 1) by Richard T. Ingram describes the 10 core areas of board responsibility.

2. *Legal Responsibilities of Nonprofit Boards, Second Edition* (Book 2) by Bruce R. Hopkins, JD, LLM, elaborates on the board's legal responsibilities, liabilities, and the oversight it should provide to protect the organization.

3. *Financial Responsibilities of Nonprofit Boards, Second Edition* (Book 3) by Andrew S. Lang, CPA, explains board fiduciary responsibilities in the areas of financial oversight and risk management.

4. *Fundraising Responsibilities of Nonprofit Boards, Second Edition* (Book 4) by James M. Greenfield, ACFRE, FAHP, helps board members understand why they should be actively engaged in ensuring adequate resources for the organization — and how to get involved in fundraising.

5. *The Nonprofit Board's Role in Mission, Planning, and Evaluation, Second Edition* (Book 5) by Kay Sprinkel Grace, MA, Amy McClellan, MNO, and John A. Yankey, PhD, shows how to define and communicate the organization's mission and link strategic planning and evaluation to achieve organizational success.

6. *Structures and Practices of Nonprofit Boards, Second Edition* (Book 6) by Charles F. Dambach, MBA, Melissa Davis, and Robert L. Gale offers guidance on how to build and structure the board (size, committees, term limits) and enhance leadership roles and the partnership between the chair and the chief executive.

Each book focuses on one topic, breaking information into manageable amounts that are easy to digest. Readers will find real-world examples that provide insight from effective boards, statistics from BoardSource's *Nonprofit Governance Index 2007* survey of nonprofit organizations, tips and pitfalls, lists of the most important things to remember, end-of-chapter questions, glossaries, and resource lists for further reading. The authors of the books are subject matter experts with years of experience in the nonprofit sector.

WHO SHOULD READ THE BOOKS?

Board members and senior staff, especially chief executives, in nonprofits of all types and sizes will find the information contained in the Governance Series relevant. They can use it to set standards, to develop their own approaches to board work and interacting with board members, and to modify practices as the organization evolves.

There's something in the Governance Series for everyone associated with the board. A board chair, for example, might share Book 5 (*The Nonprofit Board's Role in Mission, Planning, and Evaluation*) with board members before starting a strategic planning process or give Book 4 (*Fundraising Responsibilities of Nonprofit Boards*) to the development committee. Chief executives will find it beneficial to give Book 3 (*Financial Responsibilities of Nonprofit Boards*) to the board treasurer and to review Book 1 (*Ten Basic Responsibilities of Nonprofit Boards*) and give it, along with Book 6 (*Structures and Practices of Nonprofit Boards*), to senior staff and the board chair to clarify board–chief executive roles and strengthen the partnership with the board. All board members will want to read Book 2 (*Legal Responsibilities of Nonprofit Boards*) so they understand how to protect themselves and the organization. The chair of the governance committee might give new board members all six books. This sharing helps ensure that everyone associated with the board is "on the same page" and has a common understanding of the board's responsibilities, expectations, and activities.

Board service entails serious obligations, to be sure, but it can also deliver immense satisfaction. A board that knows what is expected of it and performs at the highest level is a strategic resource for its organization and chief executive. And ultimately, this commitment by dedicated board members translates into mission impact in our communities.

The Governance Series was made possible in part through the support of MetLife Foundation.

INTRODUCTION
A GREAT TRUST

Board members may think of their responsibilities in terms of how much money they should give to the nonprofit organization or what committees they will serve on. They may not realize that their responsibilities encompass far more. Ultimately, board members are responsible for the financial viability, the program success, and the very survival of the organization. Most important, for purposes of this book, they have a fiduciary responsibility.

The concept of fiduciary responsibility — a trust held for the greater community — goes back before modern times. Throughout history, from ancient Athens to the American frontier, communities have selected people to protect the common good — to make and enforce laws, spend public funds, or care for the sick.

Today's board members, as custodians of something of value to the community, have a similar role. For them, to invoke that often-quoted presidential phrase, "the buck stops here." The governing board has the ultimate responsibility for the organization's success, which includes every aspect of what happens with the organization — including the financial aspect. The board can delegate some details to a finance committee and some to an audit committee, but the full board always retains the final responsibility.

Dealing with financial matters requires board members (and staff, too) to communicate in another language. Accounting has its own vocabulary, grammar, and rules of construction. Unless you've already been trained in it, this language takes some effort to learn to speak and understand well. This book will help board members become more fluent in various aspects of accounting and thus overcome the normal "fear factor" felt by those entering this largely unfamiliar territory.

EDUCATION DISPELS FEARS

Board members must understand the issues important to financial integrity and solvency, safeguards and procedures to protect the organization, and signs of financial trouble. That means knowing how to read and understand the financial information — such as distinguishing the important numbers and relationships — and, most important, making decisions based on the information. Developing this knowledge enables board members to recognize impending problems and tell the difference between minor ripples and major crises.

Of course, a board shouldn't expect every one of its members to become a financial expert. Board members, inevitably, will have differing levels of expertise. But, at a minimum, a board should have an expert provide training so every member can attain at least a basic understanding of nonprofit accounting and the organization's financial side. In addition, all board members need to feel comfortable asking questions when they don't understand something and be able to make sense of the answers (and realize when the answer doesn't make sense). Simply put, there are no dumb questions.

Financial information is, of course, not the only type of information used in decision making. But it plays an essential part in all important decisions, even those that may, at first glance, appear non-financial in nature (for example, should we keep our clinic open an extra hour in the evening so people can get there after work?). Armed with this knowledge, decision makers can better protect and enhance the nonprofit organization's capacity to serve the community.

In 2002, after several high-profile instances of corporate financial mismanagement, the U.S. Congress passed the Sarbanes-Oxley Act. For the most part, the Sarbanes-Oxley Act does not impose legal requirements on nonprofits (two parts of it do; see pages 25-26 for more information). Its provisions (other than the report on internal controls, known as the Section 404 Report) are generally practices that nonprofit organizations should follow anyway, because doing so enhances an organization's ability to serve its constituents. Also, these good practices cost little to implement.

This book discusses these practices and other issues of importance to nonprofit organizations. For example, Chapter 1 covers general and specific financial responsibilities of boards and includes a brief discussion of the Sarbanes-Oxley Act. Chapter 2 tells who's who and defines the roles of the main players. Chapter 3 goes into more detail about internal controls and procedures, while Chapter 4 offers a primer on financial statements and audits. In Chapter 5 you'll find suggestions for dealing with outsiders who assist the organization in its financial operations, and the Conclusion provides a list of the top 10 things to remember.

Discussion questions at the end of each chapter are designed to prompt board dialogue, whether at regular times set aside on the board meeting agenda or during a special board education session on finances. Each chapter also includes several quiz questions for testing your financial literacy. Appendix I presents samples of an auditor's opinions, while Appendix II and Appendix III summarize the federal and state schedules for filing various tax and information forms. The glossary provides definitions of financial terms that nonprofit boards often encounter as they fulfill their fiduciary duty.

CHAPTER 1
FINANCIAL ISSUES BOARD MEMBERS SHOULD ADDRESS

The entire board of a nonprofit is legally responsible for the organization's financial success. This responsibility calls for the board to focus on certain areas that involve the basic financial health and welfare of the organization.

PLANNING AND BUDGETING

Many nonprofits try to do too much, with too few resources. As part of the planning process, the board should work with the staff to define the organization's mission, develop a strategic plan to fulfill that mission, and identify and implement programs to achieve the chosen strategic goals and objectives. (For more information, see *The Nonprofit Board's Role in Mission, Planning, and Evaluations*, Book 5 in the BoardSource Governance Series.)

For every activity to be undertaken, including all programs, fundraising, and general management, the plan should address the financial implications. In fact, a strategic plan that does not include an adequate financial component is guaranteed to fail. Therefore, the planning process should include

- evaluating existing and potential financial resources

- examining internal and external environmental forces affecting the organization and its funding

- reviewing the cost and effectiveness of existing programs

- examining alternatives and their financial implications

Once the board has qualitatively determined programs, timelines, and the basic scope of activities, the staff responsible for implementing the programs should develop the revenue and expense budgets needed to get the job done. Budgets should cover at least one year and preferably two years or more — although the budget for the second year need not have the high degree of detail required for the immediate year's budget. The benefits of multiyear budgeting — including a more forward-looking planning process and earlier warning of impending financial problems — easily offset the time required to implement it.

With so much at stake, the budgeting process should not be hurried. Staff should seriously consider clearly outlining all major assumptions that underlie the numbers for the board. Organizations should devote sufficient time and training to doing the job right. In fact, it may take at least six months to plan and develop a sound budget for an organization of any size and complexity; in the end, you gain a better budget, with more of the key issues worked out.

If a nonprofit organization does not have a budget, its board will have difficulty determining whether it is being managed effectively. (Most would conclude that the lack of a budget itself indicates poor management.) Simply breaking even — running at a very small gain or loss — is not enough. A budget also articulates expected performance, not only creating a goal for volunteers and employees but also providing a device for measuring success and failure.

How do you measure success? That question goes to the heart of the difference between for-profit and nonprofit organizations. A for-profit measures its financial success by how much profit it earns — the more, the better. The same cannot be said for a nonprofit organization.

Nonprofit organizations measure their success by the good they do for the community as well as how well they manage to meet (or make) their budgets. Fulfilling the mission is the bottom line; balancing the budget makes it possible.

Some organizations help balance their budget through revenue-generating activities that do not directly relate to their mission. These unrelated business activities may include selling advertising in their publications, selling general merchandise in their gift shop or bookstore, or participating in a joint venture with a for-profit organization. The organization will have to pay taxes on the net income from such activities, often referred to as the unrelated business income tax, known as UBIT. Still, it is usually better to have the net income after tax, which can be used to further the mission, than not to have the income at all. Because of the various financial and legal implications, an organization should obtain professional advice before undertaking any unrelated business activities.

TEST YOUR FINANCIAL LITERACY

Spending 72 percent of total expenses on program services and 28 percent on management and fundraising is

A. Too much on programs.

B. Too little on programs.

C. Just the right amount on programs.

D. Possibly any of the above, depending on the organization's circumstances.

Answer: D. *Although many people believe there is some "right" amount to spend on programs, every organization is different and its spending will necessarily reflect that difference. In general, it is better to spend a greater amount on programmatic activities that will help to achieve the mission of the organization, rather than on management and fundraising. In such areas as the arts, however, where fundraising can be quite challenging, these ratios may well not be as attractive. Similarly, organizations just starting out often find it difficult to maximize programmatic expenditures.*

Which of the following statements about unrelated business income is true?

A. This income is not directly related to an organization's tax-exempt purpose.

B. Because it is taxable, it should be avoided unless absolutely necessary.

C. It is usually better to have the net income after tax than no income at all.

[continued on next page]

D. Good professional advice is needed to ensure the organization is complying with tax laws.

E. All of the above except B.

Answer: E. *Taxable income is still income — and that taxable income might enable the organization to continue or expand its mission-related activities. It is perfectly acceptable for a nonprofit organization to generate revenue through activities that do not directly relate to its purpose, provided it fulfills all IRS requirements. Should this unrelated income rise to the level of 20 percent or more of the organization's total gross income, it may be wise to consider spinning off the activity into a separate taxable subsidiary. In any case, if your organization will generate any amount of unrelated income, obtain advice from professionals familiar with your type of nonprofit before undertaking the activity.*

REVENUE AND EXPENDITURES

A variety of circumstances can lead to the organization making either more or less than the amount budgeted. For example, if the organization makes more than was budgeted, perhaps it spent too little on programs or padded the budget with extra expenses just to be on the safe side. It can also mean, of course, that the organization succeeded beyond expectations in enlisting grants or other revenue.

Similarly, if the organization makes less than was budgeted, it might have taken on unanticipated tasks or allowed expenses to go out of line. Or, revenue might have fallen short of expectations. The board needs to periodically review the budgeted income and expenses and compare those figures to actual income and expenses, with staff providing explanations for significant differences. Only when it knows the full story can the board respond with appropriate action.

When the board's review indicates that the organization's expenses are rising or falling at the same pace as its revenue, the expenses are said to be "in line." Problems generally arise when expenses rise more quickly than revenue; if the organization is not already running at a deficit, then at some point it will be.

CASH VS. ACCRUAL

There are basic and subtle differences between the cash and accrual accounting methods. It is always good to remember, however, that a nonprofit should follow the Generally Accepted Accounting Principles (GAAP) when reporting its finances to the outside world.

Cash basis accounting

- Simpler and less costly

- Suitable for personal finances and for small organizations with straight-forward "money in-money out" transactions

- Expenses are recorded when a check is written; revenue is recorded when a check arrives

- Easier to follow cash flow

- May give a distorted picture if many bills are paid on time and few receivables arrive

- In general, does not reflect accurately the organization's financial health

Accrual basis accounting

- Adherence to GAAP expects accrual accounting

- Requires more detailed understanding of accounting principles

- Focuses on activity rather than when money exchanges hands

- Revenue and expenses are recorded when benefits are earned or rendered

- Does not necessarily indicate how well you manage your everyday transactions

- Gives a more complete picture of the organization's financial status

Similarly, certain items of expense directly relate to certain sources of income. For instance, it is important to ensure that publication expense is not running far ahead of publication revenue — unless the board has stated an intention to subsidize publications from other resources. There are two different and valuable perspectives to keep in mind.

The first is a programmatic perspective: Does this program's income exceed its expense? This analysis can be done at a broad level (for example, total meeting income versus total meeting expense) or at a more specific level (for example, annual meeting income versus annual meeting expense). To obtain this type of information, the organization must set up its accounting system to produce the necessary data. This calculation should include all relevant expenses, including non-cash expenses such as depreciation and expenses covered by donations. Care should be taken to include all these expenses; otherwise, the organization may believe it is making a profit in areas where it actually is not.

Of course, unlike in the business world, where profit remains the goal and the measure of success, nonprofits do not automatically change or discontinue an activity that loses money. As long as the activity in question is an important part of the organization's mission, and as long as the organization has adequate resources (such as contributions, endowment income, profits from other activities, or reserves) to draw upon to cover the loss, the board may decide to stay the course and continue the activity. But this must be a conscious decision on the board's part, be revisited regularly, and not simply be an abdication of decision making.

On the other hand, as part of its strategic planning, a board should not hesitate to pull the plug on an activity that no longer represents a significant part of the mission or when adequate resources to cover a deficit are simply not available or in prospect. Essential to any such decision is adequate, timely, relevant, and understandable financial information about the activity and about the organization as a whole.

The second perspective involves so-called natural classifications of income and expense. Examples include membership dues, interest income, and professional and maintenance expenses.

These items are more difficult to compare because they do not relate to a specific product or program but to the organization as a whole.

Nevertheless, monitoring the larger of these income and expense items in relation to each other will prove valuable. For instance, because salaries and other personnel costs (such as payroll taxes and fringe benefits) usually represent one of the largest expense areas for a nonprofit organization, the board should pay special attention to keeping them in line. To obtain a useful comparison, divide total personnel costs by total income for both current and historically comparable periods. This ratio should either improve (get lower) between periods or stay in a range appropriate to the organization. If it doesn't, the board should understand the variance.

Many different revenue and expense ratios can be computed, depending on what the organization determines is most important and meaningful. It is also possible to make comparisons with other organizations — if useful data can be obtained. This is not always easy in the nonprofit sector, although some nonprofit organizations (such as the American Society of Association Executives, Council on Foundations, and the American Hospital Association) collect and compile these financial statistics.

AVAILABLE CASH AND RESERVES

Having sufficient cash is critical to any nonprofit operation. After all, cash is the fuel on which the economic engine runs. The electric company, for instance, is unlikely to accept some of the organization's receivables, inventory, or office supplies in lieu of payment of the electric bill.

Although wide variations exist, many nonprofit organizations typically hold enough cash in a checking account to pay salaries and expenses for at least one month — or more depending on circumstances, such as the likelihood of an unexpected sudden need for cash. Mitigating factors include the ability to quickly obtain cash through the prompt sale of assets and/or gifts from one or more dependable donors. If the organization doesn't have sufficient cash in the bank, it should have liquid investments that can readily be converted into cash. Organizations that have cyclical or irregular cash flow should maintain a line of credit or other borrowing ability to ensure they have enough cash available on a year-round basis.

If an organization is short of cash, it should project the amount of cash it should have on hand at the start of each future period, how much will be received or spent during that period, and what will remain at the end of the period. Cash-flow projections should be done on a monthly basis for the ensuing 12 months, and then perhaps annually for the next two or three years. Some organizations will project weekly or even daily estimated cash on hand if they are truly cash poor. Cash-flow projections also enable the organization to plan for the purchase of new equipment, possible expansion of operations, increased staff compensation, and other essentials.

To compute a rough but useful ratio of cash on hand, take the current cash balance, subtract all bills that must be paid in the near future (each organization should define this time frame for itself), and divide the remainder by the annual budget. When the result is multiplied by 12 (number of months in a year) the answer will be the number of months that the organization could continue to operate at its currently projected level, assuming the worst case of a total cessation of income, before it would run out of cash.

Here is a hypothetical calculation:

Current cash balance	$400,000
Less bills due in near future	($100,000)
Available cash	$300,000
Annual budget	$1,200,000

Divide 300,000 by 1,200,000 = $1/4$
Multiply 12 times $1/4$ = 3 months before cash runs out

As for how much cash on hand is considered a "comfortable" amount, there is no pat answer. Each organization must make its own determination, based in part on how much of a financial cushion it maintains in the form of reserves.

Reserves contribute to a nonprofit's ability to continue performing its important services no matter what problems arise or what happens to the economy as a whole. The simplest definition of reserves, also known as the fund balance, is what remains after taking the organization's assets (or things of value it owns) and subtracting the organization's liabilities (or debts).

This simple approach, however, has several problems. Reserves are useful for such planned events as launching new programs, but they are also required when a financial crisis occurs. Inventory and fixed assets, such as furniture, equipment, or buildings, while useful, usually cannot be quickly converted to cash and thus are not likely to help resolve a crisis. On the other hand, long-term debts, such as a mortgage on a building, do not necessarily make a current crisis worse because they are paid off over a long period of time. Also, certain amounts held by nonprofits are restricted in how they may be used and will not be available in a crisis unrelated to their restricted purpose or must be kept intact in perpetuity.

Reserves might best be defined as those unrestricted assets that are reasonably liquid, minus those liabilities that must be paid off fairly soon. Therefore, a more conservative definition of reserves would be the organization's current assets (minus inventory and prepaid expenses) less its current liabilities. Organizations that have restrictions on the use of certain funds would not count such amounts as part of their available reserves.

TIP

To identify alternative sources of revenue that will help your nonprofit survive in a challenging economic environment, examine similar organizations of your type throughout your area, or the country, to determine what innovations have worked for them.

Nonprofit organizations can build their reserves only by running at a surplus, whether the surplus results from regular operations or special fundraising efforts. An organization with accumulated reserves will have funds available to invest in equipment and property, apply to program expenses, and protect the organization during periods when revenue falls below expenses. Net income builds a surplus, sometimes quickly from such events as a major fundraising campaign, but usually slowly over time.

On the other hand, some may argue, "Every dollar that hits our bottom line (that is, ends up as surplus) is a dollar that we did not use to enhance our programs." Does that mean a nonprofit organization should always just break even? Certainly not — in that case, the organization would never have any surplus, thus no financial cushion.

This save-or-spend dilemma is inherent in the concept of reserves for a nonprofit organization. Suppose the organization receives an unexpected windfall — say, a large unrestricted bequest it did not know about. The question immediately arises, "What should we do with the money?" The organization can spend it all, keep it all to earn future investment income, or spend some and keep some, in various proportions. There is usually a strong argument for spending it all right away. After all, there are always homeless people who need shelter, children who need better educational facilities, underpaid faculty who deserve a raise, a building that needs repairs, and so on.

But if the windfall is spent right away, it is gone. Next year, the same problems still exist. If the money is kept and invested, however, it will produce a perpetual stream of income that the organization can use to enhance programs indefinitely — albeit to a smaller degree. The decision about such amounts is often a wrenching one for boards because they must carefully consider competing priorities. This is part of a board's responsibility for ensuring the future of the organization's programs.

What constitutes an appropriate level of reserves will vary from one organization to the next. Too great a surplus may imply that the organization could have provided more services for the good of the community — or that it needed to raise less revenue. Neither conclusion contributes to a positive public image. Most experts agree that having one year's operating expenses in reserve puts the organization in a strong financial position. But each organization should take into account its own circumstances — considering cash flow, capital requirements, availability of outside funds in a pinch, and so forth — and set a target reserve level with which the board and management are comfortable.

Practically speaking, 35 percent to 40 percent of a year's expenses should provide sufficient breathing room for nonprofits with reasonably stable sources of income and a low probability of large unexpected needs for cash. A grantmaking foundation depends on its endowment, rather than operational reserves, to generate the cash to make grants and is legally bound to distribute at least 5 percent of its net investment assets. A small or newer operating nonprofit might well be lucky to have 10 percent to 20 percent of a year's expenses in reserve.

The concepts of endowments and reserves are often seen as closely intertwined, but they are actually two different things. "Reserves" is a term that does not have a precise meaning in nonprofit accounting but is often used loosely to refer to an organization's net assets, or some part of them, which result from the organization's accumulation of net income (excess of revenues over expenses) throughout its history. Much of this net income will often have come from operations and may be spent on any activity that furthers the organization's mission (including administrative and fundraising expenses).

However, in some nonprofits and especially in foundations and universities, donations will have been received with the specific donor stipulation that the capital must be kept for a stated period ("term endowment") or in perpetuity ("permanent" or "true endowment"), and that only the income from the capital may be spent. These donations, termed "temporarily restricted" or "permanently restricted," respectively, together with any amounts of unrestricted net assets that the governing board chooses to set aside for long-term investment purposes (sometimes referred to as "quasi-endowment" or "funds functioning as endowment"), make up the endowment of the organization.

An example of an organization that needs larger than average reserves would be an agency whose mission includes disaster relief and that is located in an area subject to earthquakes (which, by their nature, are unpredictable). This type of organization needs to carefully determine the balance between helping those in need today and ensuring that adequate funds exist for the next inevitable disaster. A university or a hospital, on the other hand, can't rely only on operational reserves but usually needs to build a permanent endowment that provides for the next generation of students or ensures that the facility remains intact to care for a continuous flow of patients.

The decision to build an endowment or rely on operational reserves for rainy days and unexpected opportunities belongs to the board. Whatever target level the board selects, the organization should build to this level over five to 10 years by funding reserves as a line item in the budget. For those organizations fortunate enough to have assets in excess of their immediate needs, or that hold donor-restricted endowment funds, the question arises of what to do with these assets — how to invest them to produce operating income, while still maintaining the safety of the principal. (See Chapters 3 and 5 for information related to investment policies and decisions.)

ENSURING APPROPRIATE ACTIONS

All organizations exist at the will of the constituents they serve. If they behave in a fashion that seems wasteful or inappropriate, the public can turn against them. Sources of funding dry up, and the organization can suffer financially or even go out of business.

The board is ultimately responsible for ensuring that the organization properly manages certain types of income. For instance, organizations that receive funding from the federal government, foundations, individual donors, or other entities must usually follow specific rules and guidelines. If they don't, they may face suspension or retraction of funding, public censure, and, in extreme cases, possibly other penalties.

Purpose-restricted grants or contributions. Frequently, donors provide funding for a restricted purpose, such as research in a specific area, a particular project, or a specific program. The organization must spend these restricted funds only for their designated purpose. Permanently restricted funds, often called endowment funds, can never be spent — only the income generated by those funds is available to spend. Nothing is more certain to damage a nonprofit organization's ability to attract funds than for it to be found using restricted funds for purposes other than those specified by the donor.

An organization that receives restricted gifts must account for the funds carefully so that it can prove their use for the purpose intended. Nonprofit organizations have developed a system called fund accounting to address the need for accountability to donors and funders and to ensure that funds are spent for their designated purpose.

Federal funding. Strict rules apply to recipients of federal funds. A substantial portion of the rules concerning what costs are allowed to be charged to federal funds appears in OMB (Office of Management and Budget) Circular A-122. Any organization expending $500,000 or more per year in federal funds is required to conduct a special audit of its handling of those funds. This is called an A-133 audit because it was communicated to the public in OMB's Circular A-133.

 PITFALL

By failing to properly use or account for the use of federal funds, your organization runs the risk of accruing severe penalties set by the federal government. Thus, before taking on federal funding, a nonprofit should make sure that its accounting system and policies are up to the task.

OMB A-133 requires that outside auditors review and report on whether the funds provided were spent for the precise purpose intended and in a fashion appropriate to all federal guidelines. It also requires the outside auditor to report on the effectiveness of the system of internal controls in ensuring compliance with federal rules and grant terms.

The federal government, through the Internal Revenue Service (IRS), also requires that the nonprofit make its annual reporting document (Form 990) available for inspection or duplication to anyone who requests it. In other words, a nonprofit's activities and finances are open to the scrutiny of volunteers, members, the media, and the public. Given this fishbowl environment, a nonprofit must not only appear to be acting appropriately but also take the appropriate actions in reality.

The appearance of propriety extends to fulfilling the organization's exempt purpose, as well as being perceived as efficiently achieving its ends. Each organization must look to others in its field to determine whether its operating and fundraising costs are reasonable in comparison. Although there are no true nationwide or industry-wide standards, each entity can be compared to its peers.

Other areas of special concern invariably include compensation and benefits to senior staff, especially the chief executive, and to officers and board members. Substantial attention by the press, Congress, and the IRS has led to stringent rules related to excessive compensation or unreported benefits. Nonprofits affected by these rules must be especially careful to operate within them to avoid penalties and to ensure they are acting appropriately. The newest version of IRS Form 990, issued for tax years beginning in 2008, includes several additional disclosures about compensation designed to add transparency to this aspect of nonprofit operations (see Chapter 4).

Excessive benefits to an officer or a board member may not come as cash compensation but instead may be hidden in such items as an above-market rental agreement with the nonprofit for property owned by the board member. Even if the board member in question was not part of the decision-making process — and thus creating a clear conflict of interest — the decision could result in an inappropriate benefit. This and similar types of arrangements can result in severe personal penalties for both the person receiving the improper benefit and the person(s) who approved the benefit — even loss of the organization's exempt status — and must be avoided at all costs. The damage resulting from even the appearance of such a relationship would be quite substantial.

TEST YOUR FINANCIAL LITERACY

Temporarily purpose-restricted net assets can always be used

A. If the board votes by a three-fourths majority to use them.

B. Only as stipulated by the donor.

C. For any purpose if there is a financial emergency.

D. Upon advice of the organization's attorney.

E. If both the board and the organization's attorney approve.

Answer: B. This is a matter of law: The organization must use contributions for purposes consistent with the donor's intent. If the organization has questions about its ability to use such funds, it should consult an attorney. A board member should remind others if they attempt to stray from the straight and narrow on this matter.

An organization should charge its federal government grants with

A. As much as it can get away with.

B. Whatever costs can't be charged to some other grant.

C. Allowable costs under OMB Circular A-122 (or A-21 if it is a college).

D. Only direct costs.

Answer: C. Charging only direct costs (D) would shortchange the organization because indirect costs are also reimbursable. A and B would serve to defraud the government, potentially subjecting the organization to exceedingly severe penalties.

AVOIDING CONFLICTS OF INTEREST

Nonprofit board members must remain vigilant in their efforts to avoid conflicts of interest — real or perceived. Even the appearance of conflict can cause significant damage to an organization's reputation.

Some of the clearest and most serious conflicts of interest occur when a staff member or volunteer influences a decision that benefits him or her financially. This can also lead to private inurement, such as a senior staff member receiving excessive compensation.

The IRS looks for private inurement when it audits nonprofits. If the IRS finds any evidence of personal gain, the recipient must return the excessive financial benefit and pay penalties. Also, the IRS may impose financial penalties, known as intermediate sanctions, on board members and managers who knowingly approved the transaction or contract.

Another example of a conflict of interest may occur when a board member is involved with a competing or potentially competing organization, either for-profit or nonprofit. It is a clear breach of fiduciary responsibility for a board member to intentionally, or even accidentally, convey confidential information to such an organization. If a situation presents the possibility that this might occur, the board member should resign one of the board positions. (See Chapter 5 for an additional discussion of contracts with outside advisors.)

Every organization should create and maintain a conflict-of-interest policy that is signed annually by all board members and senior staff and that is designed to identify potential conflicts. If a conflict arises in connection with a proposed transaction or relationship, there should be a procedure for ensuring that the matter is handled appropriately. Usually, this includes revealing the potential conflict to the board and chief executive and having the person with the conflict abstain from all discussion and voting on the transaction or relationship. Failure to have a formal policy can lead to a variety of problems.

 TIP

Once a conflict-of-interest issue has arisen, it is almost impossible to get a policy passed. Thus, a board with no existing conflict-of-interest policy should move quickly to approve one before an actual or perceived conflict arises.

A good policy should include annual reporting of actual and potential conflicts, plus a formalized process to deal with any conflicts that arise during the year. Without such a formalized process, boards often break down into angry factions, no longer focusing on what is best for the organization but taking sides with their friends. In that type of environment, an organization can accomplish little of value. (For more information on conflicts of interest, see *Legal Responsibilities of Nonprofit Boards, Book 2* in the BoardSource Governance Series.)

TEST YOUR FINANCIAL LITERACY

Buying office supplies from a board member's company is

    A. Always improper.

    B. Acceptable if the price is as low as or lower than the competition.

    C. OK if that board member abstains from discussing and voting on the deal.

    D. All right if the entire board is clearly aware of the relationship.

    E. Acceptable only when B, C, and D are all true.

Answer: E. *For a private foundation, it is simply never acceptable to do business with one of the board members; thus, A would be the correct answer. For other nonprofits, however, such a purchase is permissible if the three safeguards noted in B, C, and D are all in place.*

THE SARBANES-OXLEY ACT

In 2002, the U.S. Congress passed the Sarbanes-Oxley Act in response to several abuses in the for-profit business world. By its own terms, this federal law does not apply to organizations other than public companies — hence, not to nonprofits. However, two exceptions cause parts of Sarbanes-Oxley to apply even to nonprofit organizations. These parts prohibit retaliation against whistleblowers and prohibit alteration or destruction of documents that are relevant to a lawsuit or regulatory proceeding. Accordingly, organizations can facilitate compliance with these two provisions by having a whistleblower policy and a document destruction and retention policy.

As for the rest of the Sarbanes-Oxley Act, it sets forth a number of good practices for all organizations. These include

- having an audit committee of the board, preferably separate from the finance committee

- having at least one financial expert on the audit committee

- making the audit committee completely responsible for the relationship with the outside auditor (if one is used)

- having both the chief financial officer and the chief executive publicly attest to the adequacy and effectiveness of the organization's internal controls and the fairness of the presentation of its financial statements. Clearly, the chief executive, not just the chief financial officer, must be knowledgeable enough about the organization's accounting processes to feel comfortable making that public attestation. (See Chapter 2 for further discussion of the roles of organization leaders.)

Most nonprofits will likely not implement the provision of Sarbanes-Oxley that requires an external audit of the organization's internal controls and the issuance of an opinion. Although auditors obtain an understanding of internal controls as part of planning and performing an audit, the depth of that understanding and the amount of actual testing of the controls are not sufficient to issue an opinion on the controls. The amount of work required to issue such an opinion is quite extensive and thus quite costly. Most nonprofit organizations will likely not find it cost-beneficial to have a full internal control audit done. Of course, this does not absolve leadership of nonprofit organizations from establishing and maintaining strong internal control systems; that is a given for all organizations if they wish to retain the trust of their constituents. (See Chapter 3 for additional information on internal controls.)

Finally, Sarbanes-Oxley has affected public expectations of organizations — both for-profit and nonprofit. Donors, members, the media, regulators, and the public expect organizations to operate in a sound, ethical manner, and they will penalize those that do not by withholding contributions or memberships, by publishing critical reports, and so forth. Also, some states, notably California, have adopted laws that parallel some parts of Sarbanes-Oxley; organizations need to be aware of the state laws that apply to them.

INSURING AGAINST RISKS

Even with the greatest vigilance on the part of the board and staff, problems may arise that threaten the organization's financial health. Board members should make sure that the organization protects itself against risks, either with insurance or other means. For instance, the organization should insure its assets, have adequate protection from liabilities (including directors' and officers' insurance), and bond everyone involved with cash and securities. If being open for business is critical, business interruption insurance can provide income lost if the organization is forced to close for a time.

Risk management is not just a matter of philosophy but a bottom-line issue. As an example, one nonprofit had been scheduled to hold its annual meeting in New Orleans one week after Hurricane Katrina devastated the city in 2005. The organization did not suffer a financial catastrophe because it had insured the income from that meeting. On the other hand, another organization didn't insure its large meeting in the same city during the same week. By not exercising good risk management, the latter organization was still feeling the results of that financial loss several years later.

To help protect the organization from risks, the board should periodically review the insurance carried by the organization. If the organization has an independent auditor, the board should ask the auditor for a formal or informal opinion on whether the insurance appears satisfactory. (See Chapter 5 for an additional discussion of insurance.)

QUESTIONS THE BOARD SHOULD ASK

Planning, available cash, and reserves

1. Is our financial plan consistent with our strategic plan?

2. Are our cash-flow projections reasonable, objective, and adequate? How accurate have past projections been?

3. Do we have sufficient reserves? Has the board adopted a formal policy regarding reserves?

4. If we have permanent endowments, has the board considered a spending rate policy (spending a set percentage of the income each year) to help protect the principal?

Revenue and expenses

5. Have we run a gain or a loss — both overall and by activity? Compared to a year ago, are we better or worse off financially?

6. Do we receive management reports that identify program and non-program revenue and compare them with assigned costs?

7. Are any specific expense areas rising faster than their sources of income?

8. Do we regularly compare our financial activity with what we have budgeted? How do we make sure that the differences between budgeted and actual amounts are appropriately addressed?

9. Does the board provide oversight of contractual agreements to ensure that the organization's exempt status will not be questioned or impaired?

10. Is the organization acting in accordance with the IRS rules on executive and other compensation?

Risk, requirements, and conflicts

11. Has the board established internal controls to ensure that we appropriately spend and accurately account for restricted funding?

12. Do we provide timely reports as requested by funders?

13. Do we have a policy prohibiting conflicts of interest, and do we periodically monitor compliance with the policy?

14. Is everyone who handles cash, checks, or investments bonded?

2

CHAPTER 2
MAJOR FINANCIAL ROLES IN NONPROFITS

Nonprofits vary in size and organizational structure, but they share certain basic financial management functions. These functions include

- protecting the assets of the organization

- collecting income

- paying debts that have been properly documented

- recording receipts, disbursements, and necessary adjustments

- providing accurate, timely reports (produced within 10 days of the end of the month)

Some organizations, particularly those with exceptionally large boards, create a smaller committee, such as an executive committee, and charge it with many routine board functions. However, the full board can never delegate its overall fiduciary duty to anyone else. Every person in a leadership role — including governing board members, most committee chairs, and all senior staff — should attain a basic level of financial literacy in order to be able to assume responsibility for his or her individual financial oversight duties. This literacy encompasses the ability to read and understand financial information — both external financial statements and internal management reports — and to have some ability to sense when something is not as it should be, know when to ask questions, and understand the answers.

In addition, any middle-level staff members with the ability to commit the organization's resources must understand the financial implications of what they do. This would include people with functions such as membership, purchasing, program management, personnel, payroll, travel, investment, grantmaking, and fundraising.

Financial responsibility is generally distributed among the board and staff functions described below. The board sets policy and parameters, staff implements policy and makes recommendations, and both board and staff monitor financial performance indicators.

COMMITTEES WITH FINANCIAL RESPONSIBILITIES

Organizations often assign responsibilities and tasks for specific areas of financial performance to board committees.

Finance Committee. This committee oversees the proper performance of all the organization's financial operations by regularly reviewing all financial activity. The finance committee (or the budget committee if it is separate) reviews and discusses the budget with management before presentation to the full board. The in-depth budget review by the committee relieves the board from spending an undue amount of time analyzing details. In some organizations, this committee also reviews other financial activities such as development, employment practices, the audit, and investment performance.

Audit Committee. This committee's primary function is to accept and review reports provided by external auditors and to select the firm that will provide the next year's audit. Management should convey to the committee its assessment of the external auditor's performance. If conflicts arise between management and the auditors, the audit committee should hold a private session, without staff present, so the auditors can candidly express their concerns. (See Chapter 3 for more information on the annual audit.)

Investment Committee. This committee drafts and oversees the organization's investment policies, and acts as a liaison with outside investment advisors. Because this committee monitors investment performance, it needs members who are familiar with investing — perhaps a banker, stockbroker, professional investment advisor, or wealthy individual with experience managing a personal portfolio. In most cases, however, the committee does not become involved in the details of individual investment purchase and sale decisions because members likely do not have the time or broad expertise needed and wish to avoid any legal liability. Managing investments is what an outside advisor is hired to do. The committee should monitor the activities of an outside advisor to ensure that the organization's investment policies are being adhered to.

All financial committees of a board must exercise the same care as the full board to refrain from micromanaging the organization. Simply put, the board delegates the management of the organization to the chief executive; the board's role is to oversee. If there is no staff, the board will need to carry out more of the financial functions and pay greater attention to internal controls. However, in organizations that do have staff, attempts by the board to actually manage the organization will waste staff time and result in substantial inefficiencies. Even when embezzlement or mismanagement requires the board to take a stronger role in financial oversight, the board should work quickly to put good staff managers and solid internal controls in place and remove itself from day-to-day affairs as soon as possible.

Ideally, a majority of the members serving on these committees will be full board members. But if the organization encounters difficulty in finding enough board members for the finance-related committees, it might recruit some non-board members. Although the main benefit is to add financial expertise to a committee's work, it can also be a way of vetting potential candidates for future board membership.

TEST YOUR FINANCIAL LITERACY

The purpose of private meetings between the audit committee and the auditors is to

   A. Facilitate performance evaluation of the treasurer.

   B. Allow the auditors to raise issues with the committee without "pulling punches."

   C. Provide the audit committee with an opportunity to press the auditors for lower fees.

   D. Emphasize the independence of the committee from management.

Answer: B and D. *As B indicates, meeting privately, without staff present, encourages both the auditors and audit committee members to speak candidly about the organization's financial health and discuss options for improvement. D is also a good answer given the importance of independence in today's nonprofit environment. C is incorrect because the audit committee can press for lower prices with or without management present — although such diminution is unlikely given the increase in tasks that auditors are required to provide. A is incorrect because it is not the auditor's job to pass judgment on the performance of the treasurer.*

Board members who are not CPAs

   A. Should not serve on the audit committee.

   B. Can leave worrying about finances to the treasurer.

   C. Should resign from the board at once.

   D. Should make an effort to become more financially literate.

Answer: D. *All board members should possess some degree of financial literacy. Board education sessions — focusing, for example, on topics such as how to read the audited statements or financial trends in the nonprofit sector — help build a board's knowledge of financial issues and identify questions to ask. Thus, A, B, and C are all incorrect; a board member need not be a CPA even to serve on the audit committee. Not being CPAs, however, does not relieve board members from making every effort to fulfill their financial responsibilities to the best of their capabilities.*

TREASURER

In nonprofit organizations, the treasurer has the key volunteer financial role of overseeing financial operations. Sometimes one person holds both the secretary and treasurer positions.

Most nonprofits charge the treasurer with the legal responsibility for custody of the organization's funds and securities; keeping full and accurate account of all receipts and disbursements, the books, and financial records of the organization; and providing periodic (at least quarterly but monthly in many organizations) reports to the full board. Even in large organizations the treasurer remains legally responsible for these functions, even if a staff member rather than the treasurer performs them.

In smaller organizations the treasurer may well have hands-on responsibilities. Then, as an organization grows in size, the treasurer will transfer more functions to staff and become more of an advisor and overseer. In larger organizations, the staff assists the treasurer by doing most of the day-to-day bookkeeping, accounting, and other financial functions. As an organization grows in size and complexity, it should update its bylaws and other policy and procedure documents to reflect the changing responsibilities. The treasurer's responsibility includes ensuring that external reporting requirements imposed by funders, regulators, and others are met appropriately and on a timely basis. (Appendices II and III list the regulatory filing requirements for nonprofit organizations.)

Like other board members, the treasurer should not micromanage the financial affairs of an organization that has paid or volunteer financial staff. Budget preparation, for example, is generally a staff responsibility, although the treasurer often becomes involved well before the board reviews the document.

TIP

The treasurer must always refrain from directing or managing the organization's financial manager. That is the job of the chief executive.

Frequently, nonprofits require their treasurers to be bonded to ensure faithful performance and restoration of all books and records, vouchers, money, and other properties to the organization. Bonding is especially necessary in small organizations, where the treasurer has hands-on responsibilities.

Any other person (paid or volunteer) who has access to the organization's cash or other valuable assets should also be bonded. Then, if a misuse of funds occurs, the organization will recover its loss from the bonding company (up to the amount of the bond). A bond also helps to deter the commission of fraud because people know that a bonding company will pursue the thief and bring criminal charges, although sometimes nonprofit organizations are reluctant to do so.

CHIEF EXECUTIVE

The chief executive, in addition to running the day-to-day affairs of the organization, shares many of the treasurer's oversight duties and is responsible for hiring and supervising the head of the accounting staff. Although usually not a CPA or trained accountant, the chief executive is in charge of managing the organization and, therefore, has responsibility for its financial records. The chief executive's principal role is implementing and coordinating programs and being responsible to the board for daily administration, including staffing and operations. The treasurer, on the other hand, is more oriented toward the financial oversight functions of the board.

In all nonprofits, the chief executive has some level of contractual capability for a wide variety of financial activities, such as entering into leases, signing checks, and negotiating contracts. Frequently, there will be a cap on the level of activity that the chief executive can enter into without officer or board approval. Approval may come as a motion by the board, a sign-off by an officer, or an additional signature on a check.

The chief executive must remain conscious of the financial implications of every management decision. Almost everything the organization does is likely to either incur expenses, generate revenue, or both. Failure to consider this aspect of managing is likely to lead to decisions that are not in the best interests of the organization.

Practically speaking, the chief executive should be responsible for preparing and presenting the budget to the treasurer or to the board as a whole. The chief executive will work with staff to provide anticipated figures for revenues and expenses that are as accurate as possible. While accounting/financial personnel may assist in this process, the responsibility lies with the chief executive.

PITFALL

If the board doesn't receive financial information in a format that is readily understood, it will not have a sound basis for making financial decisions. Traditional financial statements are not as easy to absorb as graphs and charts; sometimes, narratives will be most effective. If you need help understanding financial information, ask for it!

BOOKKEEPER, CONTROLLER, DIRECTOR OF FINANCE

Which positions assist the chief executive in managing financial activity will depend on the size of the organization. The smallest organizations might simply hire a part-time bookkeeper to handle the financial record keeping. A medium-sized organization might employ a full-time bookkeeper or controller. In any case, the bookkeeper or controller is responsible for entering the financial activity, especially receipts and disbursements, into the books and records and for producing timely and accurate financial statements (monthly or perhaps quarterly).

The bookkeeper or controller is also responsible for monitoring the cash and investment accounts, making sure that the amounts reported by the banks or investment companies reconcile precisely with the records of the organization. This position usually prepares the payroll as well, although generation of checks and payroll tax returns can be outsourced.

In large organizations, the director of finance generally has several employees. For instance, a controller would be responsible for managing the financial records and tracking financial activity. The controller usually has a staff of accountants who handle accounts payable, accounts receivable, and the like. A director of finance also responsible for administration may supervise management information systems, human resources, and facilities management staff.

In all organizations, an important internal control is to segregate duties so that every transaction or activity involves two people. Obviously, larger organizations find this segregation easier to achieve, but smaller organizations should do this as much as possible. (See Chapter 3 for more information on internal controls.)

QUESTIONS THE BOARD SHOULD ASK

1. How do we divide financial responsibilities among various board committees?

2. Financially, what could go wrong in our organization? What procedures do we have in place to prevent or respond to such occurrences?

3. Does the audit committee have a private session each year with the auditor?

4. Do we have the proper staff for our financial activities?

CHAPTER 3
SYSTEMS THAT PROTECT NONPROFIT ORGANIZATIONS

The most difficult internal problems for an organization to recognize result from gradual accumulation of bad habits rather than through gross mismanagement or malfeasance. As an organization grows, seemingly insignificant erroneous activities or behaviors tend to develop incrementally. At first, they appear too small to be important. The impact of these errors can grow with the organization, however, eventually resulting in a major problem.

Certain systems should be in place to protect every nonprofit organization. Management is responsible for making sure that the organization implements and maintains these systems, but the board should ensure that management follows appropriate policies. The following systems, taken together, allow for the safe and efficient operation of the organization.

INTERNAL CONTROLS

Internal controls are those processes and procedures that protect the assets of an organization and promote its efficient operation. For example, a bill-paying process that is highly efficient, but occasionally pays invoices that should not be paid, sacrifices too much in protection of assets to achieve an otherwise valuable efficiency. The board, with the help of staff, must insist on the creation of internal controls that will meet the fundamental goal of protecting the organization's assets, thus helping to ensure its long-term stability and continuation of its programs.

Good controls act as both deterrents to, and detectors of, improper behavior by staff and volunteers. They also protect the innocent from suspicion when something improper occurs.

Sometimes staff and volunteers resist internal controls, viewing them as nuisances or impediments to getting work done. Board and senior staff may need to convince others that the benefits of strong controls outweigh the inevitable costs.

The key to good internal controls is segregation of duties — separating incompatible elements of certain transactions. The general rule is that no one person should be in a position to completely control all aspects of a transaction from its initiation through approval, handling of assets, and recording.

For instance, whoever approves invoices to be paid should not prepare checks to pay the invoices, and vice versa. Separating these functions reduces the risk of paying an inappropriate invoice. It becomes more difficult to achieve or maintain good internal controls in small organizations with fewer staff. Board members of these organizations, therefore, must work harder to gain as much asset protection as possible. Even when it is not feasible to have the strongest controls, it is usually possible to institute other procedures that mitigate a control weakness.

It is especially important to have strong controls, including adequate segregation of duties, in these areas:

- receiving and processing incoming cash — including checks and electronic transfers (with a large volume, use of a banking service such as a lockbox or caging house is often an effective control)

- processing and approving invoices to be paid and signing checks — or approving outgoing electronic transfers

- approving employee and volunteer expense reimbursement requests (no one should ever approve his or her own expense report)

- having custody of petty cash and other cash funds, such as change funds, church collections, and other gifts

- maintaining records of amounts owed to the organization (pledges and other receivables)

- approving purchases, having custody, and maintaining records of inventories of supplies and property

- having access to, and the authority to change, computer programs used to maintain accounting records

- reconciling bank and investment accounts (this is one of the most important controls, especially in the absence of other desirable controls)

- maintaining the basic accounting records (journals and ledgers)

- analyzing the variance in budgets from one year to the next

Board members should ask if the organization has an up-to-date accounting manual that details the correct procedures. If the board has any doubt about the adequacy of the internal controls, it should address questions to the external auditors. If the auditors are not reasonably satisfied with the state of the controls, the board should consider a special internal control study. Done by the outside auditors, this study involves a thorough review of the controls and results in a written report that delineates any shortcomings.

Under no circumstances should boards be lulled into believing that, just because the organization's controls are considered good, nothing bad can possibly happen. Boards must always remain vigilant to possibilities of problems. Controls can be circumvented; they can become obsolete; they cannot cover every conceivable situation.

Unfortunately, some nonprofit organizations have experienced the ill effects of inadequate internal controls. One large organization, for example, saw its chief executive go to jail for using organizational funds to pay for excessive and lavish personal travel and entertainment expenses. For several years afterward, as donors reacted to the negative publicity about the chief executive's behavior, the organization experienced a significant decline in contribution revenue — one greater in magnitude than the actual losses from the excessive expenses. Another organization that experienced a similar problem with its chief executive — and declining contributions — no longer exists.

One organization had to refund millions of dollars of federal grants when it could not document the appropriate use of the money. Yet another found itself the victim of simple embezzlement: The chief financial officer wrote and signed large checks to herself, cashed them, and covered up the missing money by making fraudulent journal entries to fix the books — a clear case of inadequate segregation of duties and weak oversight by the chief executive.

Nonprofits work hard to develop whatever assets they have. Good internal controls will help to ensure that these hard-won assets are not lost or consumed inefficiently — and it is the board's responsibility to see that this happens.

TIP

It's in the best interest of the organization to support the implementation of strong internal controls and encourage others on the board to do the same. Time and money spent to enhance controls will, in the end, enhance mission accomplishment.

ACCOUNTING POLICIES AND PROCEDURES

Every nonprofit should have written policies and procedures governing how it does business. Two documents are the most important.

Accounting manual. This written document, prepared by the accounting staff, contains the guidelines for processing transactions and maintaining good internal controls. It analyzes each step in the fiscal process and describes the appropriate procedure for handling that step. The idea is that an accountant unfamiliar with the organization should be able to come in and, without access to any current personnel, fully understand what is happening and why. (In an emergency, this may be necessary.)

The manual should indicate which staff positions are responsible for which steps in the process and even who is to substitute in case of an absence. This manual, either prepared or reviewed by professionals, should be kept up to date.

Investment policies. After the board, leadership, and staff, most nonprofits would identify cash as their most critical asset. Organizations should have procedures for safeguarding cash, for ensuring its liquidity, and for employing it productively at all times. Together, these procedures form the cash management element of the organization's investment policy.

No staff member or volunteer should have the sole responsibility for selecting investments; the board should ensure the organization abides by the board-approved investment policy. A good investment policy will

- delineate a specific philosophy of investment management and establish parameters for investment risk and return

- assist and protect the designated investment manager by setting up practical guidelines and clear performance objectives

- establish a process for regularly reviewing investment objectives and strategies and reviewing the manager's performance

Although the board is responsible for formulating an investment policy, it can — and probably should, unless it has appropriate expertise among its members — seek outside professional advice during the process.

Some policies, especially those for organizations with smaller reserves, indicate which specific investments are allowed. For example, a very conservative investment policy might allow only FDIC-insured bank accounts with balances under the $100,000 limit and short-term U.S. Treasuries. Policies for organizations with larger reserves might exclude certain high-risk investments or state what proportion of the reserves may be in stocks (equities) rather than in bonds (debt instruments). Organizations of all sizes often have a policy that requires outside advisors to select any investments that carry more risk than certificates of deposit or Treasury bills. (See Chapter 5 for further discussion of investments.)

EXTERNAL AUDITS

An audit is the process by which certified public accountants form an opinion as to whether the organization's financial statements fairly reflect its financial position, the changes in its net assets, and its cash flows. This lengthy and thorough study of the organization's financial records and procedures looks not only at the numbers themselves but also at whether appropriate accounting principles were used, and, if so, whether they were consistently applied.

Although there is no overarching law requiring nonprofits to conduct an external audit, having an audit gives the board the comfort of knowing that an outside professional has looked at the organization's books and procedures. In particular, boards of larger or more complex organizations, or those that operate many different programs or facilities in geographically diverse areas, appreciate this added comfort factor.

In some circumstances, a nonprofit organization must have an external audit. For example, an external audit may be required by

- funders, such as United Way and the federal government (if $500,000 or more of federal awards are expended in a year)

- individual states, if the organization solicits contributions from the public in the state. The majority of states require an audit of charitable organizations that solicit contributions. Thresholds that must be reached before an audit is required vary from state to state, beginning at $150,000 and topping out in excess of $2 million.

- a parent organization (if, for example, the nonprofit is a chapter or affiliate)

- a lender, if the organization has borrowed money

- an organization's own bylaws

To effectively perform this function, auditors must be absolutely independent of management. They must, by the rules of the profession, avoid financial inducements and resist pressure of any kind from management to alter their opinion. Note that an audit does not guarantee that the financial statements are perfectly accurate because it is concerned only with material or significant amounts. Nor does it ensure the competence, wisdom, or honesty of management or the long-term financial health of the organization.

PITFALL

Thinking that a financial review carries the same weight as an audit can be a problem for organizations that must meet funders' standards and donors' expectations. Before selecting a review over an audit, the board should understand precisely what is (and is not) being purchased. The assurance is *far less* than that received in an audit.

WHEN SHOULD YOU CHANGE AUDITORS?

The question of regularly changing auditors often comes up. A truly professional audit firm will maintain its perspective and independence year after year. If the board is satisfied with the audit firm's competence, independence, and perspective, it need not replace it. The audit firm's in-depth understanding of the nonprofit's operation, gained during years of auditing the organization, can be exceedingly valuable — but only when accompanied by an appropriately high level of ethics and responsibility.

Many within the nonprofit community recommend changing the lead auditor on an audit every five years. The justification for this is that anyone working year in and year out with the same organization may simply become too comfortable with the processes and systems. Changing the lead auditor and bringing in a new set of eyes introduces a different point of view without losing all of the valuable knowledge that the existing audit firm has picked up over the years.

For organizations that cannot afford a full audit, a CPA can perform a review of the financial statements. A review takes less time — and, hence, costs less — but does not provide as high a level of assurance that things are in order. Although much less thorough than an audit, a review does ensure that the financial statements have been prepared on an acceptable basis of accounting and that this year's numbers make sense given the prior year's performance. However, the inability of a review to provide substantial assurance makes it less popular with nonprofit boards and funders.

An organization may ask financially astute volunteers to undertake a members' audit. Two or more knowledgeable individuals visit the organization and test some of its fiscal activities and records, such as cash disbursements, cash receipts, whether key assets actually exist, and whether the payroll records are in good order. As with an external audit, no area of activity can be sacrosanct for a members' audit. The volunteers undertaking this effort must feel free to look where they please and be creative in their investigations. Some organizations that use member audits have an external auditor accompany the volunteers to aid or guide their efforts.

QUESTIONS THE BOARD SHOULD ASK

Internal controls

1. Do we have the appropriate checks and balances necessary to reduce the possibility of errors, fraud, and abuse?

2. If it is not feasible for us to segregate duties as much as would be desirable, how can we mitigate control weaknesses in key processes?

3. Have we adequately documented all policies and procedures related to our financial activity?

4. Do we have an investment policy? If so, are we following it?

External controls

5. Do we have an annual external audit? If not, what do we do instead?

6. Are we comfortable with the quality of service our audit firm provides, its independence, and the fee it charges?

4

CHAPTER 4
FINANCIAL STATEMENTS AND REPORTS

All board members — not just those who are CPAs or serve on the finance committee — must understand the financial condition of the organization in order to serve and protect it. Financial insight contributes to wise decision making on most board matters — even those not specifically dealing with finances.

Numerous publications can guide those not fully versed in reading and understanding financial reports. (See Suggested Resources at the end of this book for several recommendations.) Even those already skilled at reading financial statements may have difficulty understanding information offered by nonprofit organizations because accounting practices for these entities differ somewhat from accounting practices for profit-making ventures. If board members aren't satisfied with their understanding of the financial statements and explanations provided, they should ask questions until they are comfortable.

Better information can take a variety of forms. For example, because no one can absorb all the details in a financial report, communicating less (but more meaningful) information is sometimes better than simply providing detailed information with no explanation. The staff might write a narrative describing the highlights of the reporting period to accompany the financial report. Charts and graphs can help point out the most important trends or relationships. Many organizations regularly prepare and disseminate dashboard reports — quick overviews of status and overall direction. Like an instrument panel on a car, dashboard reports provide critical measures of success, which vary from one organization to the next according to what each is trying to achieve.

For a struggling nonprofit, for instance, the report might show cash on hand by month. In its dashboard report, a membership association might include new members added monthly, percentage of members retained, or total membership. A nursing facility might prefer reporting the percentage of beds occupied. In every case, the design of the dashboard should enable the viewer to know quickly which critical factors are going well and which are going poorly. Creating dashboards can be labor intensive, but they are helpful for both board and staff.

Whatever form they take, reports should be standardized so the board can quickly review and compare items with those in previous reports.

TIP

Each board member is responsible for gaining a sufficient level of comfort and understanding of the numbers. If any issue, large or small, is not clear, the board should seek clarification. A diligent board member will ask as many questions as needed to put to rest any doubts or uncertainty.

DOCUMENTS THE BOARD SHOULD RECEIVE

There is no single standard for all nonprofits regarding which financial documents the board should receive. Here are the documents a board typically reviews.

FINANCIAL STATEMENTS PREPARED FOR INTERNAL USE

Larger nonprofit organizations should prepare internal financial reports each month. While certainly needed for management, this information may not require board review. In fact, many boards find it sufficient to review quarterly internal financial statements. These internal statements do not need to be prepared on a Generally Accepted Accounting Principle (GAAP) basis of accounting, if some other basis — such as the cash basis — is considered more useful for interim periods. There is a risk, however, that boards may become confused by seeing interim statements on one basis, such as cash, and later seeing the annual audit on a different basis, such as GAAP.

In organizations with satisfactory reserves, the finance committee might analyze the monthly or quarterly reports, while the full board reviews only the annual internally prepared statement and the external audit. Boards with no finance committee should review the organization's financial statements at least quarterly.

FINANCIAL STATEMENTS PREPARED FOR EXTERNAL DISTRIBUTION

The board should always review year-end audited financial statements. If an audit has not been performed the board should review the unaudited statements. These year-end statements should include

- **A statement of financial position.** Also called a balance sheet, this statement shows the assets and liabilities of the organization at a given point in time, in this case at year-end. Whenever possible, this statement should include comparative figures from the previous year.

- **A statement of activities.** Also called a statement of revenue and expenses, this shows revenue and expenses for a specified period of time, usually one year, and whether there was a net excess or deficit for the period. This statement should include comparative figures from the previous year.

- **A statement of changes in net assets.** Previously called a statement of change in fund balance, this statement is frequently combined with the statement of activities. It reflects the beginning net assets, plus the current period's excess or deficit, and may include other adjustments to reach the ending net assets.

- **A statement of cash flows.** This document focuses on where cash came from and how it was used. It can be a good early warning sign of an impending cash crisis. (This statement should not be confused with the internal cash-flow statement discussed in Chapter 2, which is a tool for managing cash.)

In addition to these statements, every group of audited financial statements must be accompanied by footnotes that help the reader understand the organization's financial situation. Board members should read these footnotes carefully. The notes highlight significant accounting policies, major acquisitions or changes in operations, pension requirements, lawsuits, and details on other significant matters.

On occasion, management or the board of an organization will want more detailed information — such as additional details of expenses or details of information by individual program or fund — than is required in the basic audited statements. In these situations, the auditors will attach to the report a separate opinion, followed by additional statements or supplemental schedules. This opinion will indicate the level of assurance the auditors are providing on this information, which may differ from the level of assurance provided for the basic audited statements.

OPINIONS

Various types of opinions may result from an audit. Most organizations receive a clean (or unqualified) opinion, but some do not. Listed below are the different types of opinions and why they might be received (Appendix I includes an example of each).

- **Unqualified (clean) opinion.** This, the highest level of assurance the auditor can provide, is used when the auditor is satisfied with the financial statements. It typically includes three paragraphs, although a few audit firms use one paragraph. This type of opinion sometimes includes an additional paragraph drawing the reader's attention to a particular matter. This paragraph follows the opinion paragraph of a clean opinion. It does not reduce the level of assurance the auditor is expressing; it simply refers to the full disclosure of the matter in question in the footnotes at the end of the financial statements. Examples include opinions based in part on the work of another auditor or emphasis on a matter such as the unknown outcome of a pending lawsuit.

- **Qualified opinion.** This is provided when the auditor expresses reservations on a specific issue. Qualified opinions result when the organization is following accounting principles that are not generally accepted, according to the

American Institute of Certified Public Accountants, or when the auditor was unable to complete all of the audit work deemed necessary to issue an unqualified opinion. A qualified opinion should encourage board members to ask questions directly of the auditors.

- **Adverse opinion.** This is a negative opinion, issued when the financial statements are misleading and management will not correct them. These are exceedingly rare and should alert the board to the need for strong corrective action.

- **Disclaimed opinion.** This indicates that the auditor is unable to form an opinion. It may arise because of a lack of independence or because of a scope limitation, meaning that the auditor has been unable to gather enough information to form an opinion. This type of opinion can also result when the organization's internal controls are unsatisfactory. When a board receives a disclaimed opinion, it should promptly investigate the cause of the disclaimer.

In addition to providing an opinion on the financial statements, auditors generally provide a management letter, sometimes called an internal control letter. The board should always receive this document, which provides the auditor's observations on any control deficiencies, significant deficiencies, or material weaknesses discovered in the internal control structure of the organization during the audit. Significant deficiencies represent serious matters, and material weaknesses are very serious matters. Both require the board's immediate attention, followed promptly by corrective action.

In addition, the management letter may mention other matters that the auditor believes are sufficiently important to require the chief executive's attention. If the auditor does not discover any reportable matters, no written communication is issued.

PITFALL

If the board accepts the auditor's report without each member reading the management letter, it may overlook material weaknesses and other problems noted by the auditors. The board should schedule follow-up reporting by management to determine that the problems have been effectively resolved.

Form 990

In addition to the nonprofit organization's audited financial statements and the management letter, the federal and state governments, grantors, donors, or affiliated organizations may request to see the organization's Form 990. This annual report, filed with the IRS, provides information about the organization's revenue, expenses, assets, and liabilities and explains its mission, major program areas, and governance practices.

For the 2008 tax year, the federal government substantially revised the IRS Form 990 for the first time since 1979. The greatly expanded form includes a variety of new schedules and areas of focus. In addition, the IRS readjusted the requirements for filing this form and the less complicated Form 990-EZ and now requires even the smallest organizations with gross income under $25,000 to file a simple electronic postcard.

 PITFALL

Ignorance about the IRS requirements for annual filings will not prove to be an effective defense mechanism. Failure to file a Form 990, the simpler Form 990-EZ, or the Form 990-PF for private foundations is cause for automatic loss of tax exemption. Board members should make it their responsibility to ensure the organization files one on a timely basis.

Smaller organizations have to be particularly wary. In tax years ending on or after December 31, 2007, tax-exempt organizations whose total income is normally $25,000 or less are required to electronically submit Form 990-N, also known as the e-Postcard. While there are some exceptions for churches and their related entities, as well as organizations that file in group returns, this filing is quite important since an organization that fails to file the Form 990-N for three consecutive years will automatically lose its tax-exempt status.

The new Form 990 has a substantially revised summary page that gives a quick snapshot on the organization's mission, major programs, and key factors about the composition of the board.

Part VI (Governance, Management, and Disclosure) is of particular interest to board members. The questions it contains represent an effort by the IRS to either encourage appropriate behavior or reveal inappropriate behavior. Part VI is divided into three Sections:

Section A, Governing Body and Management, includes questions that ask

- the number of voting members of the governing body and how many of those are independent

- whether any officer, director, trustee, or key employee has a family or business relationship with any other officer, director, trustee, or key employee. The IRS is looking for an entangling web of control that can turn a nonprofit into a vehicle for personal gain.

- if the organization has delegated control over management duties customarily performed by or under the direct supervision of officers, directors or trustees, or key employees to a management company or other person. This question probes whether an outside company or individual is receiving undue profit.

- whether there was any significant change to the organizational documents during the year

- whether the organization became aware that it had a material diversion of assets during the year

- about contemporaneously kept records of the meetings and actions of the governing body in and each committee that can act on behalf of the governing body

- whether the organization has local chapters, branches, or affiliates. If yes, the form asks whether written policies and procedures govern the activities of such chapters to ensure that their operations are consistent with those of the organization.

- whether a copy of Form 990 was provided to the organization's governing body before the form was filed. In Schedule O, all organizations must describe the process, if any, the organization uses to review the form.

Section B requires you to note whether your organization does or does not have certain policies. Questions ask

- whether the organization has a written conflict-of-interest policy. If the answer is yes, the next question inquires if officers, directors or trustees, and key employees are required to annually disclose interests that could give rise to conflicts and whether the organization regularly and consistently monitors and enforces compliance with the policy. The process then must be described in Schedule O.

- about the existence of a written whistleblower policy

- about the existence of a written document retention and destruction policy

- about compensation for senior executives. The IRS provides safe harbor procedures to help see that key employees are not being overpaid; if followed, they can be described on Schedule O.

- whether the organization has entered into business with a for-profit entity during the previous year

Section C is largely interested in such straightforward matters as which states the Form 990 is filed in and whether it is available online. One question asks the organization to describe whether (and, if so, how) the organization makes its governing documents, conflict-of-interest policy, and financial statements available to the public.

Based on the details now required on Form 990, most organizations want to ensure they can answer the questions the way the IRS prefers. In any event, the policies being encouraged by the IRS are good for the organization. Board members should review the Form 990 before it is filed, not only because the IRS suggests this but also because this document communicates to the IRS how the organization is fulfilling its tax-exempt purpose.

The IRS also requires nonprofit organizations to make the Form 990 available for inspection or duplication to anyone requesting access to it. Thus, accurate and effective communication is essential to maintaining a positive public image of the organization. If the organization makes its Form 990 widely available — on its own Web site, for example, or on a public Web site such as GuideStar — then it may refer requestors to that posting. The organization, however, must still comply with any requests to inspect the form in person.

OTHER FINANCIAL REPORTS

The finance or audit committee should also review the reports from the OMB A-133 audit, which is required for organizations expending $500,000 in federal funds in a single fiscal year. In a series of up to five separate reports, the auditor must attest to the fact that there is "reasonable assurance that the organization or institution is managing federal awards in compliance with applicable laws and regulations."

Whether or not board members review other required year-end reports is largely a matter of the report's significance to the organization. Whenever a report involves the potential of substantially increased or reduced funding, for example, board review is advisable. Reviewing insignificant reports, however, draws time and attention away from other matters. Board members should focus their attention where it will do the most good.

TEST YOUR FINANCIAL LITERACY

Improper financial management practices always include

A. Operating with a deficit budget.

B. Failing to file IRS Form 990 on a timely basis.

C. Not distributing financial information to the board until three months after the end of the period.

D. Both A and B.

E. Both B and C.

Answer: E. *Deficit budgets (A) are not a sin — as long as the organization has adequate reserves to draw on. Accumulating large reserves is not inherently bad, provided the organization has a sound reason for having them, such as being financially prepared for the loss of a major revenue source or for an unexpected investment opportunity. Failure to file the IRS Form 990 on a timely basis and failure to distribute financial information to the board until three months after the end of the period clearly indicate that financial records and reports are not being maintained in a businesslike fashion. Also, by failing to file the 990 on a timely basis, the organization brings itself to the attention of the IRS and may subject itself to audit, as well as penalties and interest for late filing. Finally, not providing the board with timely financial information increases the likelihood that important decisions are being made in the absence of the underlying facts — clearly a dangerous situation.*

An organization receives 70 percent of its revenue from one donor. It

A. Should ask this donor to give less so it won't be so dependent.

B. Should cultivate additional revenue sources.

C. Can only hope it is included in the donor's will.

D. Should budget only 30 percent of what it would like to spend each year in case this donor dies.

Answer: B. *Relying on one donor to provide a majority of income places the organization in a precarious financial position if that donor withdraws the support. Diversifying revenue sources, such as by adding new products or services, or entering new markets, provides a broader base of support and thus greater financial security.*

TEST YOUR FINANCIAL LITERACY

If the management letter contains material weaknesses, this means

    A. The organization needs to make office repairs and improvements.

    B. The organization's programs are inappropriate.

    C. The organization has significant problems in internal controls.

    D. Top management is doing an excellent job.

Answer: C. *If an auditing firm mentions material weaknesses in its management letter, it has identified substantive problems with how the organization handles its finances internally. Such a determination calls for immediate corrective action to be taken. Material weaknesses are exceedingly important and related to internal controls, so A and B are irrelevant to the issue. D is incorrect because the opposite situation exists; material weaknesses indicate that top management has allowed a serious problem to arise.*

Which of the following could be considered an indication of organization success?

    A. A medical research organization goes out of business after finding a cure for the disease.

    B. A graduate of the university wins the Nobel Prize.

    C. There is a waiting list for season tickets to the theater.

    D. Alumni of the halfway house have a 40 percent lower recidivism rate than is typical.

    E. All of the above.

Answer: E. *All of the answers are valid because every nonprofit must determine its own measurements of success. Note, however, that these answers all involve data related to mission or programs rather than finances. An organization might also want to include financial indicators, such as amount of reserves or end-of-year surplus, when determining what success looks like.*

SIGNS OF FINANCIAL DISTRESS

Certain occurrences portend trouble. An organization that has neglected to pay employment taxes or is teetering on the edge of bankruptcy, for example, may have few options for getting back on firm financial footing and have to close its doors. Long before reaching that point, however, an organization typically gives off distress signals to which board members should remain alert. Signs of organizational distress include the following:

Decline in critical income sources. Every nonprofit organization relies on certain major sources of income. A membership organization, for example, may rely on dues, meeting income, education, or publications as its key sources. A charitable organization's revenue may come primarily from contributions, from foundations, or from government grants. The board should carefully track income from these key sources because any significant decline points to trouble in the future.

Although an organization may appear, on the surface, to be financially sound with a healthy surplus, its expendable resources may not be adequate to cover a significant decline in income. This can occur because the organization has tied up many resources in illiquid assets such as property, receivables, or inventory. Another possibility is that most of the resources are donor restricted and therefore cannot be used for general operations.

In particular, boards must understand the difference between donor-restricted endowments and quasi-endowment (or board-designated endowment) funds. Because quasi-endowment funds are legally unrestricted, the board can use them for any purpose. Such funds, however, can provide income in perpetuity, so a board should carefully consider whether depleting them for a short-term fix is in the organization's best long-term interest.

Increase in certain expenditures. Certain expenses require more scrutiny than others in nonprofit organizations. The most important of these are salary and benefits, which represent a major portion of the organization's expenditures. Nonprofit organizations use benefits as an incentive somewhat more frequently than do for-profits, and tracking these expenses as a percentage of total expenses can be illuminating.

One expense that tends to indicate problems is the miscellaneous expense account. If this item increases, hidden costs or less-than-adequate bookkeeping may be the cause. In either case, the situation warrants an inquiry. Another expense to watch is consultants' fees. If this expense goes up noticeably, it may reflect activity that could be better brought in-house. In addition, a rise in consulting or legal costs can signal an undisclosed major issue.

Private inurement. When the IRS audits a nonprofit organization, it invariably attempts to ferret out incidents of private inurement, or private benefit. If it finds any appreciable amount, it can revoke the entity's tax-exempt status. Examples of private inurement include excessive compensation, buying or selling of assets at prices unfavorable to the organization, loans on terms unfavorable to the organization, and the like.

The only people who should gain financially from a nonprofit organization are those it employs — and the benefit they receive should only take the form of reasonable salary and benefits. (Rarely will a nonprofit organization compensate its board members with a salary or any type of benefits.) All others who receive benefit should do so as a result of the organization fulfilling its exempt purpose.

Unplanned auditor turnover. If the external auditor resigns from the assignment, this may indicate a substantial disagreement between management and the auditing firm. Or, it may point to financial problems within the organization, which the board must promptly identify and address.

The board, either directly or through its finance or audit committee, should hold a private meeting with the auditors without management present. Upon investigating the situation, the board may find it simply a matter of the organization's inability or unwillingness to pay a fee that the auditor finds satisfactory. Whatever the case, the board needs to understand the reasons behind the auditor's departure.

Board micromanagement. When there is an appropriate level of staff, good board members can focus on the big picture and minimize their involvement in operational management. A board that becomes involved in many small-dollar decisions creates enormous inefficiencies.

Micromanagement generally arises when a board has traditionally received too much detailed financial information on an ongoing basis — in a real sense, it has been trained to micromanage. Weaning the board away from this level of detail and encouraging its members to adopt a strategic focus can be difficult but is essential. By concentrating on the details, the board loses its ability to focus on the risks facing the organization and to identify the strategies to survive in a rapidly changing world. The board must seek a broader overview, such as a dashboard, to tell it that all is well or to identify any problem areas.

The other leading cause of micromanagement is embezzlement. Once the board becomes aware of this type of loss, no matter what the amount, it inevitably goes into micromanagement mode. After all, the loss occurred on the board's watch. Once the organization has taken corrective measures, however, board members must put the matter behind them and return to their strategic work. True leaders will encourage others to move on — the organization's staff has real work to do, and so does its board.

QUESTIONS THE BOARD SHOULD ASK

Financial documents

1. Do financial staff members provide accurate and timely financial statements that enable us to understand the financial state of the organization? If not, how could the statements be improved?

2. Do most board members feel that they can at least reasonably understand the financial statements? If not, how can we improve our board's comprehension?

3. Does our annual audit have a clean opinion? If not, why not? What have we done to address the issues raised by the auditor?

4. Do we annually review the Form 990? Does it accurately represent our organization?

5. Do we file, on a timely basis, all the reporting documents required by law?

Financial distress

6. Are our key sources of income rising or falling? If they are falling, what are we doing about it?

7. Are our key expenses, especially salaries and benefits, under control?

8. If we have had unplanned auditor turnover, what were the reasons for it?

CHAPTER 5
DEALING WITH THE OUTSIDE FINANCIAL WORLD

Board members who aren't experienced in financial matters often become uncomfortable when faced with major decisions that have long-term financial implications for a nonprofit. They may not feel qualified, for example, to select a bank or insurance provider, choose appropriate places to invest, or identify the most appropriate types of insurance.

Typically, the organization's staff handles the details of establishing and maintaining the relationships discussed below. Still, the board — or an appropriate board committee — should always review and approve all such contracts before they are signed and monitor the relationships to ensure satisfactory performance. Staff may also wish to involve a board member — for example, the treasurer — when establishing the relationship. Of course, in smaller organizations with few staff, board members may need to become deeply involved in such matters.

CHOOSING A BANK

When making this critical decision, the organization should select a sound and stable financial institution that is both experienced with and comfortable serving nonprofits. To bankers, especially lenders, nonprofits substantially differ from for-profit organizations. To find a bank that understands how nonprofits operate, contact other nonprofits in the community for recommendations.

Not all banks provide similar services, so the board should identify the organization's needs and approve the selection of a bank that can meet them. Every bank offers common services, such as accepting deposits and paying on checks, but look for other features such as lockbox services and payroll processing. Many nonprofits also want advice on handling investments, a service frequently available from banks today.

Although most banks have lending programs, some are not interested in lending to nonprofits, especially those without assets to pledge as security. This unwillingness to lend can be a problem, since nonprofits frequently have cyclical income. For instance, cash flow may increase around the time of an annual fundraising event, at the end of the year when taxpayers make last-minute tax-deductible contributions, or during membership renewal season. Many nonprofits rely on the availability of a line of credit to even out fluctuations in their cash flow.

Establishing a good banking relationship is an important part of a nonprofit's financial life, especially if the organization needs refinancing of a long-term debt or a line of credit that it may borrow against from time to time. Thus, before switching to another financial institution, negotiate with the current bank about key services required.

TIP

Select a bank with a branch near the organization's offices to minimize travel time. Many nonprofits make daily deposits, and other transactions may require a trip to the bank, so convenience counts.

OBTAINING INSURANCE

The insurance requirements of nonprofits are similar to those of other types of organizations, with several significant differences. Insurance needs vary based on the nonprofit's size, wealth, and types of activities. Other nonprofits can recommend agents or brokers with substantial nonprofit experience who can provide details about the alternatives.

All organizations large enough to have an office should have basic insurance coverage as provided in the standard office liability package. Such coverage includes property insurance, which protects against loss due to damage or destruction of real property, furnishings, and equipment. The policy should cover property belonging to others who may be on the organization's premises as well as the nonprofit's property when in outside locations or in transit. A good property insurance policy will cover damaged or lost property for its replacement value rather than its original cost or some other figure.

A standard office liability package also includes protection against claims for bodily injury or property damage resulting from the nonprofit's activities. Generally, this coverage applies to activity conducted on the organization's property, except that certain activities — such as provision of medical care — require separate malpractice liability insurance. Also, any time that an organization's activities involve children, it will need adequate protection from claims of improper behavior by organization personnel.

In addition to the basic office liability package, nonprofits should consider

- bonding for employees and volunteers who handle cash or securities

- coverage for art or other unique items on the organization's premises. These items generally require a floater on the basic property insurance policy.

- coverage for papers and records, both electronic media and hard copy

- convention cancellation and interruption insurance to protect against loss of income from special events or major conferences. There are well-documented incidences of earthquakes or violent storms preventing events from taking place. Without insurance, the nonprofits would have suffered financially.

- auto insurance, if the organization owns vehicles. They must be insured for all drivers, including volunteers.

- Directors' and officers' (D&O) liability insurance, which protects the organization's volunteers from suits brought by dissatisfied members of their community or people outside the organization who believe the volunteers have behaved inappropriately. (Note: D&O applies only to board members and other volunteers who receive no compensation.) D&O

insurance should cover legal fees as well as successful claims against the organization. Although nonprofit organizations frequently win these cases, the legal costs of defense can be very high, which makes this insurance worthwhile. It is especially important for organizations that provide any kind of medical care or work with children.

Maintaining a higher deductible can help keep premiums low. Issuing a competitive request for proposal (RFP) can also contribute to finding the best value in insurance. Before purchasing insurance, read the policies carefully to confirm the coverage being obtained. If no board or staff member has the expertise to understand the details of each policy, then seek additional assistance, either paid or volunteer. The organization should review its insurance policies at least every two years. (For more information on insurance and other risk management strategies, see *Legal Responsibilities of Nonprofit Boards*, Book 2 in the BoardSource Governance Series.)

TEST YOUR FINANCIAL LITERACY

General liability insurance

> A. Should be maintained by every organization.
>
> B. Is cost-effective only for larger organizations.
>
> C. Is needed only if children are involved in organization activities.
>
> D. Protects against medical malpractice.
>
> E. All of the above except D.

Answer: A. *By purchasing general liability insurance, an organization can protect against loss stemming from damage or destruction to property, equipment, furnishings, and personal property of people on its premises. In addition, general liability insurance usually covers any injuries sustained by volunteers, employees, or others while on the organization's premises or attending an event sponsored by the organization. B is not correct because general liability insurance can be purchased quite reasonably by all sizes of organizations. C and D are also incorrect because they raise irrelevant qualifications.*

MAKING INVESTMENTS

In the investment area, a nonprofit's foremost concern is ensuring it has sufficient cash available to operate. The initial available funds should be maintained in a bank account, usually a checking account, insured by the Federal Deposit Insurance Corporation (FDIC).

When funds begin to accumulate, other interest-bearing bank accounts are generally the first investment made. Such accounts should be monitored to make sure that they remain within the $100,000 range of FDIC coverage. When investable funds pass that point, the next move is often to U.S. Treasury securities. Although they lack some liquidity, U.S. Treasury securities not only are the most secure investment available but also provide a better yield than bank accounts.

With an additional accumulation of assets, the board should consider broadening the investment alternatives. The first step is to identify the operating cash that the organization needs (see Chapter 1) and keep it in readily accessible bank accounts. The remaining funds are then placed in short-term or long-term investment vehicles, in keeping with the investment policy approved by the board (see Chapter 3).

Short-term investments should be made with an eye toward high liquidity because they may be needed at any time. It is important to preserve capital while seeking the best return possible, commensurate with the need for liquidity. Short-term investment vehicles include U.S. Treasury and other U.S. government agency obligations, certificates of deposit (but not in excess of the FDIC limit), money market accounts (especially those backed by the U.S. Treasury), and more exotic items such as repurchase agreements (with U.S. government obligations as collateral). All these investments are secure and reasonably liquid.

For long-term investments of funds not expected to be used in the near future, the goals should include growth equal to or preferably in excess of inflation. With these types of investments, expect fluctuations over the short term. Long-term investment planning frequently focuses on allocating assets among stocks, bonds, and some cash. The exact mix should be expressed in an investment policy developed and approved by the board of directors, usually with the assistance of outside investment advisors.

A long-term portfolio can include a variety of investments. Equity investments may include both small-capitalization and large-capitalization stocks. Large-cap stocks are from corporations such as General Electric, IBM, and Microsoft. A small-cap stock has greater risk but greater potential for reward. Some nonprofits also include international stocks in their portfolios. On the fixed-income side, most nonprofits purchase high-quality U.S. corporate bonds. Some may add riskier, higher-yielding bonds and perhaps international bonds or so-called "alternative investments" such as hedge funds, venture capital funds, or real estate.

Diversification is a key strategy when building a long-term portfolio. The spread of investments among stocks, bonds, and cash protects the organization from substantial diminution of its capital over an extended period. Generally, nonprofits avoid speculative investments such as commodities, derivatives, or on margin.

If the organization is a private foundation under the Internal Revenue Code, special rules apply to its investing activities. These rules include, among other things, a limitation on the percentage of voting stock of a corporation that could be held by a private foundation, as well as a limitation on investments that are deemed excessively risky. The foundation should be certain that its investment advisors are familiar with these rules and adhere to them.

PITFALL

When selecting an investment advisor, any candidate related to a senior executive or a board member personally or through business would raise a red flag. This type of a relationship could create a serious conflict of interest. If the organization can afford it, hire an expert to select investment managers.

CONTRACTS WITH OUTSIDE ADVISORS

In most cases, staff will handle the process of identifying and selecting an accountant, tax lawyer, banker, insurance broker, or other expert professional. The board remains responsible for approving and selecting the external auditor. For all but the smallest and most routine contracts, however, the governing board should establish procurement guidelines and perform the final contract review and approval.

When looking for a particular type of advisor, start by contacting other nonprofits. Good, current references enable the staff and board to consult other organizations that have worked with the prospective advisor in the same capacity. It is also a good idea, and an inexpensive safety check, to contact the Better Business Bureau or local consumer affairs office when dealing with a consultant new to the organization. That step may identify whether the individual or company has a reputation for having problems.

The organization's formal agreement with the advisor identifies the elements of the relationship. At a minimum, the agreement should include statements or descriptions of the following:

- the services to be provided

- a designated nonprofit contact

- a timeline, including milestones to measure progress

- a confidentiality clause, if appropriate

- costs (and how they are computed)

- the payment procedure and schedule, including progress billing

- the form of the final work product

- the ownership of any intellectual property rights that may be involved

- the stipulation that final payment is predicated on the organization's satisfaction with the work performed

- penalties for failure to perform, including indemnification for resulting losses

- the ability to extend the agreement if mutually desired

- the termination notice period and penalties, if any

The agreement must state specifically that the advisor is an independent contractor, not an employee of the organization, and as such has full responsibility for personal income taxes, Social Security taxes, and insurance. Draft agreements may be available from the organization's attorneys. Before any agreement is finalized, an attorney should review it to ensure that the organization is well protected.

QUESTIONS THE BOARD SHOULD ASK

Banking

1. Are we satisfied with the services our bank currently provides?

2. When did we last check to see if our banking costs are appropriate?

Insurance

3. Have we thoroughly reviewed our operation to make sure we are appropriately insured?

4. Do we have directors' and officers' liability insurance?

Investments

5. Do we make sure that no board or staff member is individually responsible for selecting investments?

6. Are we satisfied with the performance of our investments given the level of risk appropriate for these funds?

Outside advisors

7. Do we have appropriate contracts with all of our current outside advisors?

8. What procedures do we have in place to make sure that all outside advisors will sign an appropriate contract before they work for us in the future?

CONCLUSION
TOWARD A BETTER BOARD

A well-functioning nonprofit organization provides services or products of such great importance that the community dedicates time and money to help it achieve its purpose. Board members are custodians not only of the organization's assets and liabilities, but also of the accumulated efforts of those who preceded them in founding and expanding the entity they now serve. In any challenging economic climate, it is essential that board members focus on this aspect of their duties. No matter what the mission of the nonprofit, the organization will be successful only if financial underpinnings remain sound. Board members must maintain a close eye on the financial direction of the organization, and its economic stability, if they are to truly fulfill their fiduciary responsibility and pass on an even stronger organization to future boards.

TEN THINGS TO REMEMBER

Board members hold in trust the economic engine that is the nonprofit's ability to continue to serve the community. To protect and enhance this organizational capacity, keep the following points in mind:

1. Never lose sight of who your customers are. You may refer to them as patients, clients, students, concertgoers, members, or parishioners; in some cases, your customers are the general public or other nonprofit organizations. They are the reason your organization exists. But, in many cases, they are not the sole source of your revenue.

2. Make your first loyalty to your customers, your second to the organization that serves them. Sometimes you'll need to make tough choices when those two loyalties come into conflict. (For example, should you spend every dime now

to provide more service or keep some in reserve for tomorrow or a rainy day?) Your third loyalty is to your donors; if you don't keep them happy, they will not return.

3. Take the business of being a board member seriously. It is not a job for the faint-hearted or lazy. You are responsible for the organization's success or failure. If the organization fails, the customers will lose — and, in many cases, the customers can least afford to lose. And you certainly don't want a failure to occur on your watch.

   Alternatively, if all seems well, do not relax and assume everything will continue that way. Hard times often follow good times, so boards must always prepare for a change in circumstances and remain strategic when making decisions that will affect the organization's future.

4. Develop some degree of financial literacy. You can't expect the treasurer (or accountant or chief financial officer or CPA) to take sole responsibility for looking after the money. The board has the fiduciary responsibility to become and remain informed. If at any point you do not understand the organization's financial condition, work with someone who does until you are more comfortable with numbers.

5. Assume that fraud and other illegal activity could happen in your organization. Some in the nonprofit sector view internal controls and procedures as nuisances or impediments to efficiently and effectively serving clients. Without good controls, however, an organization might not survive and its clients would then lose out on the services it provides. Management and the board must establish and maintain good controls; that is not the auditor's function.

6. Model ethical, honest, transparent, and accountable behavior. Sharing information not only inspires confidence among volunteers, staff, and donors but also makes them feel involved and included in the organization's mission and activities.

   Even more so than customers of a business, stakeholders of a nonprofit are sensitive to negative publicity about their organization, such as revelations of fraud or mismanagement. And these same volunteers, staff, and donors will head for the door if arguments develop over a conflict of interest; after embezzlement and private inurement, the thought that someone is taking undue advantage of the organization greatly concerns the community.

7. Obtain competent professional advice when necessary. The board doesn't have to know all the answers, but it must make sure to ask for them. Knowledgeable attorneys, accountants, tax advisors, consultants, fundraisers, investment advisors, insurance agents, bankers, and the like can provide the information the board needs to make sound decisions.

8. Comply with all tax laws. Being tax exempt does not give a nonprofit organization the license to avoid compliance. Nonprofits — and their managers and board members, personally — can get into trouble if they forgo paying employment taxes, withholding Social Security taxes, paying tax on unrelated business income, filing Form 990 on a timely basis, and numerous other requirements.

9. Resist the temptation to jump in and manage the organization. That's what you hire the chief executive (or recruit volunteers) to do. The board's role is planning, oversight, and fundraising — not getting involved in operational details. The board should step in only if problems become evident (unless, of course, the organization does not have a paid staff).

10. Regularly assess the areas of risk related to the organization. No organization operates without risks; by identifying these risks, you can mitigate them before they hurt the organization and, thus, the people it serves.

Your efforts on behalf of the organization constitute a valuable service. The nonprofits that serve the United States and the world today could not deliver their valuable services and products without the contribution of the time and effort of their boards. So take satisfaction and pride in what you do — the world is a better place for it.

APPENDIX I
EXAMPLES OF AN AUDITOR'S OPINIONS

A. An unqualified or clean auditor's opinion as recommended by the American Institute of Certified Public Accountants:

INDEPENDENT AUDITOR'S REPORT

Board of Directors
XYZ Nonprofit Organization, Inc.
City, State

We have audited the accompanying statement of financial position of the XYZ Nonprofit Organization, Inc. (the Organization), as of December 31, 2008 and 2007, and the related statements of activities, changes in net assets, and cash flows for the years then ended. These financial statements are the responsibility of the Organization's management. Our responsibility is to express an opinion on these financial statements based on our audits.

We conducted our audits in accordance with auditing standards generally accepted in the United States of America. Those standards require that we plan and perform the audit to obtain reasonable assurance about whether the financial statements are free of material misstatements. An audit includes examining, on a test basis, evidence supporting the amounts and disclosures in the financial statements. An audit also includes assessing the accounting principles used and significant estimates made by management, as well as evaluating the overall financial statement presentation. We believe that our audits provide a reasonable basis for our opinion.

In our opinion, the financial statements referred to above present fairly, in all material respects, the financial position of the XYZ Nonprofit Organization, Inc., as of December 31, 2008 and 2007, and the results of its operations and its cash flows for the years then ended, in conformity with accounting principles generally accepted in the United States of America.

Auditing Firm Name
City, State
April 21, 2009

B. Following are four samples of language variations based on non-clear opinions.

QUALIFIED OPINION

Qualified for accounting (final paragraph of auditor's report): "[In our opinion...present fairly], except that [item] is not presented fairly...." The presumption here is that the improper item(s) is/are significant but not pervasive. In other words, a reader can still rely on the rest of the information in the statements. There will be a description of the incorrect item(s) and their significance.

Qualified for scope (first and final paragraphs of auditor's report): "[We have audited the statements], except that we were unable to audit [item]....[In our opinion...present fairly], except for any adjustments that might have been necessary if we had been able to audit [item]." Again, the presumption is that the rest of the information has been satisfactorily audited.

ADVERSE OPINION

The final paragraph of the auditor's report would begin, "In our opinion...the statements do not present fairly...."

DISCLAIMER OF OPINION

The final paragraph of the auditor's report would begin, "We are unable to give an opinion on the financial statements...."

EMPHASIS OF A MATTER

One of the above forms of opinion, to which is added brief explanatory language about a matter of importance that the auditor believes the reader should be aware of. An example might be an uncertainty (see previous item) that was not significant enough to warrant a disclaimer of opinion but still important enough to warrant special attention. The exact language will vary depending on the nature of the matter being emphasized.

APPENDIX II
FEDERAL TAX AND INFORMATION FILING CALENDAR FOR NONPROFIT ORGANIZATIONS

Filing	Form	Due Date*
Initial Formation		
• Application for Employer Identification Number	SS4	ASAP after formation
• Application for Recognition of Exemption		
501(c)(3)	1023	15 months after formation
Other than 501(c)(3)	1024	15 months after formation
Payroll Forms and Returns		
• Unemployment Tax	940/940EZ†	1/31
• Social Security and Withholding Tax	941	4/30, 7/31, 10/31, 1/31
Information Returns		
• Wages and Tax Statements	W-3/W-2	2/28, 4/1 if e-filing
• Miscellaneous Income Statements	1099MISC	2/28, 4/1 if e-filing
• Interest Income Statements	1099INT	2/28, 4/1 if e-filing
• Other Income	1099 Series	2/28, 4/1 if e-filing
• 1099 Transmittal	1096	2/28, 4/1 if e-filing
• Exempt Organization Returns	990	5½ months after end of fiscal year

(Note: Some larger organizations are required to file this form electronically. Smaller organizations may file Form 990-EZ instead. Very small organizations (those with budgets under $25,000) are required to electronically file Form 990-N, often referred to as an "E-Postcard," and private foundations must still file the 990-PF.)

- Group Exemption
  Update (List)   9/30 for upcoming year

- Exempt Organization
  Business Tax   990-T   5/15

- Estimated Payments   3/15, 6/15, 9/15, 12/15

Political Action Committee

- Initial Registration   8871   24 hours after the
                         date it is established

- Interest Income   1120-POL   3/15

- Employee Benefit Plans   5500   7/31
  (Pension, 401(k); Health, Group Life, Disability, or Dependent
  Care; Group Legal Services or Educational Assistance; Cafeteria
  Plans)

APPENDIX III
STATE TAX AND INFORMATION FILING CALENDAR FOR NONPROFIT ORGANIZATIONS

FILING	DUE DATE* (varies by state)
Initial Formation	
• Combined Registration Application	ASAP after formation
• Application for Exemption	ASAP after formation
• Charitable Solicitation Registration‡	ASAP after formation
Payroll Forms and Returns	
• Unemployment Tax†	4/30, 7/31, 10/31, 1/31
• Payment of Taxes Withheld	20th of month (varies by state)
• Annual Reconciliation and Report of Withholding	1/31
Personal Property Tax‡	varies by locale
Sales and Use Tax§	varies by locale
Report of Unclaimed Property	11/1
Annual Corporate Report	4/15 (varies by state)
Copy of Federal Form 990	5/15 (not required by all states)
Corporate Income Tax Return	1/31
• If Organization Receives Unrelated Business Income	3/15 (varies by state)

- Estimated Payments   3/15, 6/15, 9/15, 12/15

Charitable Solicitation Annual Report‡   5/15

Political Action Committee

- State Election Reports (election year)   4/15, 7/15, 10/15, 1/31

- Corporate Income Yax (on interest income)   3/15
  (varies by state)

*Based on tax and plan years ending December 31

†501(c)(3) organizations may be exempt

‡501(c)(3) only

§501(c)(3) may apply for exemption

GLOSSARY

Accrual accounting — Accounting method that recognizes transactions when they occur, rather than when cash is received or paid. (Contrast with Cash-basis accounting.)

Amortization — The process of allocating the original cost or fair value of a long-lived intangible asset over its estimated useful life. (See Depreciation.) Conceptually, depreciation and amortization are the same thing. In practice, depreciation is most often used with tangible assets, and amortization with intangible assets and liabilities.

Annuity gift (gift annuity) — A contribution given on the condition that the recipient organization make periodic stipulated payments to the donor or other designated individual. After termination of the stipulated payments, the organization keeps the remaining principal of the gift.

Asset — Something of value owned or controlled by a person or organization.

Audit — The procedures performed by an independent certified public accountant (CPA) to be able to give an opinion that an organization's financial statements are fairly stated in all material (significant) respects.

Audit committee — A committee of the board whose primary function is to accept and review reports provided by external auditors and to select the firm that will provide the next year's audit.

Bonding — A type of insurance recommended to have in place covering all volunteers and employees who have access to the organization's cash or other valuable assets. If a covered individual misuses of funds, the organization will recover its loss from the bonding company (up to the amount of the bond).

Cash-basis accounting — Accounting method that recognizes transactions only when cash is received or disbursed. (Contrast with Accrual accounting.)

Cash flow — The process in which cash is received and disbursed by an organization. Most nonprofits have a cyclical cash flow with a larger influx of cash based on year-end contributions or prior to the annual meeting, and significantly lower receipts at other times of the year. As a result good managers of financially weaker nonprofits will be quite familiar with the cash flow pattern of their organization and plan expenditures accordingly.

Conditional promise to give — A promise to give that depends on the occurrence of a specified future and uncertain]qui vide] event to bind the promisor. (See Donor-imposed condition.)

Conflict-of-interest policy — A written document intended to ensure that decisions made about an organization's operations and the use of its assets are made solely with the best interest of the organization in mind, and that no private or personal benefit to any affiliated individual will result. All board members and key employees should be cognizant of the conflict-of-interest policy, and annually disclose whether they have any "interests that could give rise to conflicts" (IRS 990, Part VI, Section B, 12b).

Consolidated financial statements — Financial statements that include added-together financial information for two or more related entities.

Contribution — An unconditional transfer of cash or other assets to a qualified tax-exempt organization (or a settlement or cancellation of its liabilities) in a voluntary nonreciprocal transfer by another person or entity. (Contrast with Exchange transaction.) Contributions include gifts of money, property, the use of property, and services of volunteers; unconditional promises to make gifts in the future; and bequests.

Custodian fund — Funds received and held by an organization as a fiscal agent for others.

Dashboard report — A report that communicates critical information in a concise, visual, more compelling way than traditional narratives or financial statements. This type of reporting allows leaders and managers to focus on key trends and relationships that are fundamental to the success of the organization.

Deferred gift — A gift whose benefit to the nonprofit recipient is delayed until a later time. (See Split-interest gift.)

Deferred revenue — Revenue received in one accounting period that, because it has not yet been earned (by the provision of goods or services to the payor), is recognized in a later accounting period when the goods or services are furnished. Example: A theater subscriber pays for season tickets in June for the season starting the following September. As of June 30, the theater records the revenue as deferred until the season when the plays will be performed.

Depreciation — The process of allocating the original cost of a long-lived tangible asset over its estimated useful life. (See Amortization.) Conceptually, depreciation and amortization are the same thing. In practice, depreciation is most often used with tangible assets, and amortization with intangible assets and liabilities.

Designated fund(s) — Refers to unrestricted resources that the board has voted to set aside for a period of time or for a specific use. While the board may use the term Endowment fund, because the restriction was set internally, the funds can be made available by the board for any use at any time. Hence, board-designated funds are correctly classed with unrestricted net assets.

Directors' and Officers' Insurance — A policy that protects the board and officers if they are acting responsibly by covering a variety of potential vulnerabilities, including libel and slander, acts beyond granted authority, wrongful termination and/or discrimination, inefficient administration or waste of assets, and the like.

Donor-imposed condition — A donor stipulation that specifies a future and uncertain event whose failure to occur releases the promisor from the obligation to transfer assets (or gives the promisor a right of return of any assets it has already transferred).

Donor-imposed restriction (related to temporary restriction) — A donor stipulation (q.v.) that specifies a use for a contributed asset that is more specific than broad. A restriction on an organization's use of the asset contributed may be temporary or permanent.

Donor-restricted endowment fund — An endowment fund created by a donor stipulation that requires investment of the gift in perpetuity or for a specified term. (See Endowment fund.)

Endowment fund — An established fund of cash, securities, or other assets to provide income for a nonprofit organization. The use of the assets of the fund may be permanently restricted, temporarily restricted, or unrestricted. Restricted endowment funds are established by donor-restricted gifts and bequests to provide a permanent endowment (a permanent source of income) or a term endowment (income for a specified period).

Exchange transaction — A revenue transaction related to the provision by an organization of goods or services to customers in exchange for payment of approximately commensurate value. (Contrast with Contribution.)

Expenses — What an organization spends in the conduct of its activities (for example, salary, office supplies, rent).

Fair value — The amount at which an asset could be bought or sold in a current transaction between willing parties — that is, other than in a forced or liquidation sale; usually equivalent to market value.

FASB (Financial Accounting Standards Board) — The private sector body primarily responsible for setting generally accepted accounting principles (GAAP) for all nonprofit and for-profit entities other than governments.

Fiduciary — A person entrusted with management of, and responsibility for, assets belonging to others. Generally, under state laws, governing boards of nonprofit organizations are considered to be acting as fiduciaries.

Finance committee — Oversees the proper performance of all the organization's financial operations by regularly reviewing all financial activity. The finance committee reviews and discusses the budget with management before presentation to the full board. The in-depth budget review by the committee relieves the board from spending an undue amount of time analyzing details. In some organizations, this committee also reviews other financial activities such as development, employment practices, the audit, and investment performance.

Financial statements — Reports indicating the economic condition and financial performance of an organization. These may include a statement of financial position, also called a balance sheet, which shows the assets and liabilities of the organization at a given point in time; a statement of activities, also called a statement of revenue and expenses, which shows revenue and expenses for a specified period of time; a statement of changes in net assets, previously called a statement of change in fund balance, this statement is frequently combined with the statement of activities, and reflects the beginning net assets, plus the current period's excess or deficit; and a statement of cash flows, which focuses on where cash came from and how it was used over a period of time. If the financial statements have been audited, they will include an opinion by the auditor as well as footnotes providing significant additional information about the organization.

Fixed assets — Land, buildings, vehicles, equipment, and similar assets with an extended useful life.

Form 990 — The Internal Revenue Service (IRS) form used to report annually to the IRS (and to many states) on the financial and other activities of a tax-exempt organization.

Functional expenses — A method of grouping expenses according to the purpose for which costs are incurred. The primary functional classifications are program expenses, fundraising expenses, management, and general expenses. (Contrast with Natural expenses.)

Fund — An accounting entity established to track the resources of a specified subpart of an organization, such as a project, donor-restricted gift, board-designated pool of assets, activities in a certain geographic area, fixed assets, or other defined unit.

Fund balance — The excess of assets over liabilities of a particular fund of an organization. (See Net assets.)

Fundraising expense — Expenses incurred to induce donors to make contributions to an organization.

GAAP (Generally Accepted Accounting Principles) — The rules for recording and reporting transactions in financial statements. In the United States, these are promulgated primarily by the Financial Accounting Standards Board and secondarily by the American Institute of Certified Public Accountants (AICPA).

GAAS (Generally Accepted Auditing Standards) — The procedures undertaken by an independent certified public accountant in order to issue an opinion on the fairness of the presentation of financial statements. In the United States, these standards are promulgated by the AICPA.

Gift-in-kind — A contribution other than cash or marketable securities. Includes property, supplies, equipment, use of property (free rent), and qualified donated services of volunteers.

Grant — Properly used to refer to an award by a foundation, company, nonprofit organization, or government agency to an organization or individual. The word does not have a precise meaning in accounting and is often used interchangeably with contribution; however, not all grants are contributions — some are exchange transactions.

In-kind donation — See Gift-in-kind.

Internal controls — Those processes and procedures that protect the assets of an organization and promote its efficient operation thus helping to ensure its long-term stability and continuation of programs. Good controls act as both a deterrent to, and detective of, improper behavior by staff and volunteers. The key to good internal controls is segregation of duties. The general rule is that no one person should be in a position to completely control all aspects of a transaction from its initiation through approval, handling of assets, and recording.

Intermediate sanctions — Penalties that may be imposed by the IRS when it finds any evidence of inappropriate personal gain (termed private inurement) in a nonprofit that it is auditing. In these cases, not only must the recipient return the excessive financial benefit and pay penalties, but the IRS may impose financial penalties on board members and managers who knowingly approved the transaction or contract.

Investment committee — Drafts and oversees the organization's investment policies, including liaison with outside investment advisors. Because this committee monitors investment performance, it needs members who are familiar with investing. In most cases, the committee does not become involved in the details of individual investment purchase and sale decisions but hires outside advisors to do so. The committee should monitor the activities of the outside advisor to ensure that the organization's investment policies are being adhered to.

Investment policy — A board-approved document that delineates a specific philosophy of investment management and establishes parameters for investment risk and return. Some policies, especially those for organizations with smaller reserves, indicate which specific investments are allowed. For example, a very conservative investment policy might allow only FDIC-insured bank accounts with balances under the $100,000 limit and short-term U.S. Treasuries. The policy should assist and protect designated investment managers by setting up practical guidelines and clear performance objectives. It should also establish a process for regularly reviewing investment objectives and strategies and reviewing the manager's performance.

Joint costs of multipurpose activities — Costs incurred in an activity that includes at least two different types of functional expenses (most often, program and fundraising components). Organizations mailing requests for contributions that also educate potential donors must take exceeding care in appropriately splitting the costs of such mailings between the two functions.

Liability — An enforceable present obligation to transfer assets or provide services to another person or organization. For example, the amount owed to a vendor for products received is a liability.

Management and general expense — Expense other than program, fundraising, or membership development. Includes expenses for oversight, business management, general record keeping, budgeting, financing, and related administrative activities.

Management letter — Sometimes called an internal control letter. A communication from the organization's auditor that the board should always receive following an external audit, it provides the auditor's observations on any control deficiencies, significant deficiencies, or material weaknesses discovered in the internal control structure of the organization during the audit. Significant deficiencies represent serious matters, and material weaknesses are very serious matters. Both require the board's immediate attention, followed promptly by corrective action.

Membership development expense — Expenses incurred to induce new members to join a membership organization.

Members' audit — A process used to provide limited assurance to the membership in which two or more financially astute volunteers visit the organization and test some of its fiscal activities and records, such as cash disbursements, cash receipts, whether key assets actually exist, and whether the payroll records are in good order. As with an external audit, no area of activity can be sacrosanct for a members' audit. The volunteers undertaking this effort must feel free to look where they please and be creative in their investigations. Some organizations that use member audits have an external auditor accompany the volunteers to aid or guide their efforts.

Natural expenses — Classification of expenses by categories such as personnel costs, occupancy, travel, supplies, and professional fees. (Contrast with Functional expenses.)

Net assets — The excess of assets over liabilities of a fund or an entire organization. Net assets may be categorized as unrestricted, temporarily restricted, or permanently restricted. (See Donor-imposed restriction.)

Not-for-profit organization (essentially equivalent to nonprofit) — An entity that possesses the following characteristics that distinguish it from a business enterprise: (a) contributions of significant amounts of resources from resource providers who do not expect commensurate or proportionate pecuniary return, (b) operating purposes other than to provide goods or services at a profit, and (c) absence of ownership interests like those of business enterprises. Not-for-profit organizations have those characteristics in varying degrees. Organizations that clearly fall outside this definition include all investor-owned enterprises and entities that provide dividends, lower costs, or other economic benefits to their owners, members, or participants, such as mutual insurance companies, credit unions, cooperatives, and employee benefit plans. (See Tax-exempt.)

Nonprofit organization — See Not-for-profit organization.

Nonreciprocal transfer — A transaction in which an entity incurs a liability or transfers an asset to another entity (or receives an asset or cancellation of a liability) without directly receiving (or giving) value in exchange. (See Contribution.)

OMB Circular A-133 — Publication of the U.S. Office of Management and Budget, which requires that organizations spending $500,000 or more of federal grants and contracts in a year have a special audit of those federal funds. (See the Circular for precise definitions.)

Operational reserves — See Reserves.

Permanent restriction — A donor-imposed restriction stipulating that resources be maintained permanently but permitting the organization to use or expend part or all of the income (or other economic benefits) derived from the donated assets.

Permanently restricted net assets — The part of the net assets of a nonprofit organization resulting from contributions and other inflows of assets whose use by the organization is limited by donor-imposed stipulations that neither expire by passage of time nor can be fulfilled or otherwise removed by actions of the organization.

Plant fund — An accounting unit (see Fund) used by some organizations to record transactions related to land, buildings, vehicles, and equipment.

Prepaid expense — An expense paid in one accounting period, where the benefit of the expense is not yet received by the organization paying it, and recognition is delayed until a future accounting period after the benefit of the expense is received. Example: A rent payment for January is made before the end of the preceding December and thus is correctly classified as a prepaid rent.

Private inurement — Improper receipt of a financial benefit by a person who is an "insider" to a nonprofit organization. Insiders include members of the governing board and senior management, close members of their families, and other organizations with which they are connected. Illegal under Section 501(c) of the Internal Revenue Code, private inurement can lead to financial penalties against both the receiver of the benefit and the persons in the organization who authorized the benefit, along with possible loss of tax-exempt status.

Program expense — An expense that directly or indirectly supports specific activities constituting an organization's purpose(s) or mission(s) for which it exists. (See Supporting expense.)

Promise to give — A written or oral agreement to contribute cash or other assets to an entity. A promise to give may be either conditional or unconditional. The word *pledge* is often used interchangeably.

Quasi-endowment fund — Unrestricted endowment. (See Endowment fund.)

Reclassification — The movement of resources between classes of net assets. The most frequent reclassification is movement from temporarily restricted net assets to unrestricted net assets upon the fulfillment or expiration of a donor-imposed temporary restriction.

Restricted support — Donor-restricted revenues from contributions that increase either temporarily restricted net assets or permanently restricted net assets. (See Unrestricted support.)

Restriction — See Donor-imposed restriction.

Reserves — Not a precisely defined term, but often used to refer to the amount of resources currently available to an organization to use in any way it chooses (presumed to be limited to activities consistent with its mission.) Many in the nonprofit industry define reserves as being the equivalent of net assets (i.e., assets minus liabilities). This, however, fails to take into account the fact that reserves should be available to be spent in a time of need. Thus the figure should not include illiquid assets such as land and buildings, nor be reduced for such long-term debts as mortgages. In precise accounting terms, reserves might be more accurately defined as the unrestricted net asset balance less equity in property and equipment, plus the expendable temporarily restricted net asset balance, plus the deferred revenue that will become available within one year.

Revenue — Technically, income from providing goods or services to customers (clients, patrons, members, and so forth) and from other earning activities such as investments. Practically, is frequently used to include both earned income (from exchange transactions) and income from contributions.

Sarbanes-Oxley (SOX) — A law passed by the U.S. Congress in 2002 in response to abuses in the for-profit business world. While generally applicable to public companies, SOX requires that nonprofit organizations have and ensure compliance with policies that prohibit retaliation against whistleblowers and prohibit alteration or destruction of documents that are relevant to a lawsuit or regulatory proceeding. In addition, SOX sets forth a number of good practices for all organizations, such as having an audit committee (with at least one financial expert) that is completely responsible for the relationship with the outside auditor.

Spending rate — One method of computing the amount of investment return to be considered as available for current use under the "total return approach." (q.v.)

Split-interest gift — General term used to describe various types of gifts under which the benefit of the resources involved is split between the donor (or other designated person) and a charity. Includes gift annuities, remainder trusts (annuity trusts and unitrusts), lead trusts, and pooled income funds.

Stipulation — An expression by a donor, in connection with a contribution or a promise to make a contribution, constituting a condition, a restriction, or both. (q.v.)

Supporting expense — Expenses other than program expenses. Supporting expenses include management and general, fundraising, and, for a membership organization, membership development expenses.

Tax exempt — Literally, statutorily exempt from tax. Often erroneously used interchangeably with not-for-profit; the two terms have completely different meanings, although in practice they overlap considerably.

Temporarily restricted net assets — The part of the net assets of a nonprofit organization resulting from contributions and other inflows of assets whose use by the organization is limited by donor-imposed stipulations that either expire by passage of time or can be fulfilled and removed by actions of the organization pursuant to those stipulations.

Temporary restriction — A donor-imposed restriction that permits the donee to use up or expend the donated assets as specified and is satisfied either by the passage of time or by actions of the organization.

Term endowment — Temporarily restricted endowment. (See Endowment fund.)

Total return approach — A method of managing endowment assets in which a portion of capital gains is made available for current use under a formula approved by an organization's governing board.

Treasurer — The key volunteer financial role involving overseeing financial operations. Most nonprofits charge the treasurer with the legal responsibility for custody of the organization's funds and securities; keeping full and accurate account of all receipts and disbursements, the books, and financial records of the organization; and providing periodic reports to the full board. In smaller organizations, the treasurer may well have hands-on responsibilities; in large organizations, the treasurer remains legally responsible for these functions, even though a staff member rather than the treasurer performs them.

Uncertain — Less than likely. Judgment is often required to assess whether the probability of an occurrence should be considered as uncertain versus likely.

Unconditional promise to give — A promise to give that depends only on passage of time or demand by the promisee for performance. (Contrast with Conditional promise to give.)

Unrelated business income (UBI) — Income from a trade or business, conducted by a tax-exempt organization, that is not substantially related to the purposes for which the organization is exempt. Net income from such a business is taxable. (See Internal Revenue Code Sec. 512 and 513 for the precise definition.)

Unrestricted net assets — The part of net assets of a nonprofit organization that is neither permanently restricted nor temporarily restricted by donor-imposed stipulations.

Unrestricted support — Revenues from contributions that are not restricted by donors. (Contrast with Restricted support.)

Whistleblower — An employee, former employee, volunteer, or member of an organization who makes a good faith effort to disclose improper activities to those who have the power to take corrective action. The misconduct may be a violation of state or federal law, rule, or regulation; theft or misuse of organization funds; gross misconduct or inefficiency; or any condition that may significantly threaten the health or safety of employees or the public.

SUGGESTED RESOURCES

Berger, Steven. *Understanding Nonprofit Financial Statements, Third Edition.* Washington, DC: BoardSource, 2008.

The newly revised and expanded edition of this best-selling title brings an understanding to key accounting terms and concepts, important benchmarking ratios, and sample nonprofit financial statements. Steven Berger's no-nonsense explanations are helpful for board members, treasurers, finance committee members, and staff who prepare financial information for the board.

BoardSource. *The Nonprofit Board Answer Book, Second Edition: A Practical Guide for Board Members and Chief Executives.* Washington, DC: BoardSource, 2007.

The second edition of this best-selling, indispensable resource contains 80 questions and answers — a wealth of information about board structure and process, meetings, board composition, orientation, board-staff relations, financial management, and much more. The book offers insight gained from hundreds of board self-assessments and questions and challenges from thousands of nonprofit leaders. Written in an easy-to-use questions-and-answer format, it includes action steps, examples, and worksheets.

Butler, Lawrence M. *The Nonprofit Dashboard: A Tool for Tracking Progress.* Washington, DC: BoardSource, 2007.

Dashboard reports communicate critical information to your board in a concise, visual, more compelling way. Dashboards help nonprofit leaders focus attention on what matters most in their organizations. This book, for board members and senior staff, presents different options for creating dashboards and offers detailed illustrations and considerations. To help organizations get started with their own dashboard reports, the accompanying CD-ROM includes a dashboard generator file with two different customizable dashboard templates and how-to instructions for working with the file.

Fry, Robert P. *Minding the Money: An Investment Guide for Nonprofit Board Members.* Washington, DC: BoardSource, 2004.

Minding the Money will introduce your organization to the current investment world of hard-won dollars and will involve nonprofit board members in investment planning in a non-intimidating way. With action questions, helpful tips, and real-life case studies, readers will understand difficult financial concepts they can implement in their own board service. A customizable CD-ROM offers practical appendices, including sample policies, self-guided investment audits, and Web links to applicable state statutes.

Lawrence, Barbara, and Outi Flynn. *The Nonprofit Policy Sampler, Second Edition.* Washington, DC: BoardSource, 2006.

The Nonprofit Policy Sampler is designed to help board and staff leaders advance their organizations, make better collective decisions, and guide individual actions and behaviors. This tool provides key elements and practical tips for 48 topic areas, along with more than 240 sample policies, job descriptions, committee charters, codes of ethics, board member agreements, mission and vision statements, and more. Each topic includes anywhere from two to 10 sample documents so that nonprofit leaders can select an appropriate sample from which to start drafting or revising their own policy. All samples are professionally and legally reviewed. Samples are included on CD-ROM.

McLaughlin, Thomas A. *Financial Committees*. Washington, DC: BoardSource, 2004.

Accountability is increasingly important to nonprofits, and every board must be engaged in understanding its fiduciary duties. Learn about the core responsibilities finance, audit, and investment committees can hold. Discover how these committees can address challenges in helping the rest of the board understand complicated fiscal issues. This book will also help finance committees to stress the importance of board member independence in oversight and audit functions, and prepare the board to address potential new legal regulations.

ABOUT THE AUTHOR

ANDREW S. LANG, CPA

Andrew Lang is president of LangCPA Consulting, LLC, a firm located in the Greater Metropolitan Washington area specializing in creative solutions for nonprofits. Lang is a nationally recognized expert who has dedicated his 35-year career to helping nonprofits improve their practices to be able to better serve their members and fulfill their missions.

Lang has a variety of specialties based on his unusual combination of a strong financial background, his expertise as a communicator, and his absolute dedication to ethical behavior. Best known for his ability to identify and implement additional revenue opportunities, including rationally raising dues and smoothly adjusting pricing, he is also widely recognized for assisting nonprofits in making difficult decisions when challenging financial or operational issues require a truly independent third party. Another specialty involves his ability to redesign financial communications so non-financial people can understand them.

Among the organizations he has served as a consultant are the National 4-H Council, American Institute of Certified Public Accountants, American Society of Association Executives, United Way, American Nurses Association, Goodwill Industries International, National Association of Counties, and National Science Teachers Association, to name just a few.

Lang's professional teaching and writing include educating thousands of nonprofit executives and volunteers, writing hundreds of articles, and authoring or co-authoring nearly a dozen texts. His recent work in these arenas includes creating and presenting Lang Learning's course on Optimizing Your Financial Leadership Team, which enhances trust and effectiveness between an association's volunteer and executive financial leadership. Lang also created and presents the top two financial courses for the American Society of Association Executives (ASAE): Financial Management for CEOs and Maximizing Non-Dues Revenue. Lang's articles most frequently appear in association industry publications such as *Associations Now* and *Association Trends*.

Lang has been active in numerous organizations that serve the nonprofit community. He served 11 years on the American Institute of CPA's (AICPA's) Annual Not-for-Profit Industry Conference Planning Committee, the last three years as chairman. He has also been a member of numerous professional committees, such as the AICPA Governmental and Not-for-Profit Expert Panel and the ASAE Finance and Business Operations Section Council. In 2008, Lang was appointed to the board of governors of the Greater Washington Society of CPAs for a three-year term.